Not My Turn
to Die

Not My Turn to Die

Memoirs of a Broken Childhood in Bosnia

Savo Heleta

⁴AMACOM

American Management Association

New York • Atlanta • Brussels • Chicago • Mexico City
San Francisco • Shanghai • Tokyo • Toronto • Washington, D. C.

Special discounts on bulk quantities of AMACOM books are available to corporations, professional associations, and other organizations. For details, contact Special Sales Department, AMACOM, a division of American Management Association, 1601 Broadway, New York, NY 10019. Tel: 212-903-8316. Fax: 212-903-8083.
E-mail: specialsls@amanet.org
Website: www.amacombooks.org/go/specialsales
To view all AMACOM titles go to: www.amacombooks.org

Library of Congress Cataloging-in-Publication Data

Heleta, Savo, 1979–
    Not my turn to die : memoirs of a broken childhood in Bosnia /
Savo Heleta.
        p.   cm.
    ISBN 978-0-8144-0165-1
    1. Yugoslav War, 1991–1995—Children—Bosnia and Hercegovina.
2. Children and war—Bosnia and Hercegovina. 3. Yugoslav War,
1991–1995—Bosnia and Hercegovina—Personal narratives, Bosnian.
4. Heleta, Savo, 1979–   5. Bosnia and Hercegovina—History—
1992–   I. Title.
DR1313.7.C56H45 2008
949.703092—dc22
[B]
                                                    2007045696

Printing number

10 9 8 7 6 5 4 3 2 1

This book is dedicated to Daniel Whalen.
*The world would be a much better place
if there were more people like him.*

Acknowledgments

I can never give enough thanks to Daniel Whalen, who gave me an opportunity to go to college and pursue my dream.

Thanks to all my professors and fellow students at the College of Saint Benedict and Saint John's University in Minnesota, for inspiring me to think big and believe that, with hard work, everything is possible.

I would like to give special thanks to my English professor, Sarah Pruett. Without her, I would never have been able to read, write, and speak English.

I would like to thank my friends Michael Young, Joe Neznik, Jason Hardie, and Michael Scharenbroich for persuading me during our study-abroad trip to South Africa in 2005 to write about my wartime experience in Bosnia.

Special thanks go to Michael Scharenbroich and his family. In their home in Minneapolis, I wrote the first draft of my book. Thank you for your kindness, help, and support, and for believing that I could write a book!

I am grateful to Tunie Munson-Benson! Without her guidance, support, and help, I would never have finished the book. She always believed this was meant to happen.

Many people have read sample chapters and contributed with their feedback, comments, and questions to the final text. I would like to give special thanks to William Graves, Maria Carrow, Father Don Talafous, and Professor Cynthia Curran.

Thanks to my friend Russel Younglao for helping me to come up with the title for this book.

I am grateful to my Bosnian friends Vanja Sinanovic-Absmaier, Sanja Djermanovic, Aleksandar Bundalo, Samir Omerefendic, Kristina Seslija, Damir Tokic, Marina Maric, Adem Lisicic, Dusan Kosic, and many others for their support. Many thanks to Christina Fesler, Carol Yamasaki, Kathy McGonaglek, and Addy Spitzer for all their help and support.

I have been fortunate to have Maryann Karinch as my agent and Christina Parisi as my editor. Their questions, comments, and passionate work greatly improved the manuscript. I would like to thank Andrew Ambraziejus and the entire AMACOM team for all their work and effort in publishing my book. Also, thanks to Barbara Chernow and Chernow Editorial Services for their work on my book.

Special thanks to Jade Peterson, whose love and support make life and work so much more interesting and fun.

And finally, thanks to my parents, sister, and extended family, for their advice, support, and love.

Acknowledgments

Author's Note

My intent in writing this book is not only to expose what people did to my family during the war; it is also to show the way to peace. It is to show that even when you live through the nightmare that happened to me and my family, it is still possible to forgive and to reach reconciliation.

The events described in this book are accurate as far as I remember them and a true account of what happened to my family during the Bosnian war. But I have changed the names of the majority of people involved to protect their privacy. I know they, like me, have begun to rebuild their lives, and I don't want to interfere with this process.

The names of my family members, Slobodanka Adamovic, Mitar Puhalo, Vlado Nedimovic, Daniel Whalen, and Sarah Pruett were not changed.

Prologue

*T*he Muslim drivers looked terrified, their hands on the steering wheels and their eyes riveted to the bumpers in front of them. They were driving through enemy territory after almost four blood-soaked years, and here they'd been stopped in the middle of nowhere due to some formalities.

It was a foggy, rainy day in the spring of 1996. The war had ended only months before, and this was one of the first convoys going to the Bosnian capital of Sarajevo to get food for Goražde. No one would guarantee the safety of the Muslim drivers, so the NATO peacekeeping forces agreed to escort the convoy. If someone wanted to attack the drivers, a dozen NATO soldiers assigned to protect them wouldn't be enough to save them, just as the UN had not been able to prevent and stop the war and the loss of one hundred thousand lives.

With nothing else to do, my friends and I had decided to walk the length of the convoy, looking for familiar faces.

"Wait a second. I recognize that man," I said to my friends.

I pointed to a man in his forties who sat in the cab of a truck.

"He's probably someone who lived in your neighborhood before the war," one friend said. "Or maybe he's the dad of some kid you knew."

"No, this is different. I have a really bad feeling about this guy." I stared at the truck. Unshaven and with hefty bags under his drawn and hazy eyes, the driver looked as if he hadn't slept for days.

"Let's keep going," my other friend called over his shoulder as he walked on. "I want to see if we know anyone."

As we walked from truck to truck, it came to me.

"I have to go back! I think he is the man who tried to kill my family!"

I ran back to the truck. Another close look at that face and my head and heart began throbbing. At first, I couldn't believe he would have the guts to come here. Could it really be him?

I recognized that face. It was him!

My anger bubbled up from deep inside. This man, sitting safely inside his muddy truck, had brutally terrorized my family. We'd stayed in Goražde when the war began. As Serbs in a Muslim-controlled city under siege, we'd had reason to fear for our lives, both because of the relentless Serbian attacks on the city and because of our ethnic differences from the people in charge. The Muslim majority saw us as the enemy within their city walls, not victims of the same guns that were killing their families.

I wanted to open the door, drag him to the ground, and strangle him. I tried to open the truck; the door was locked.

"Get out!" I yelled in rage.

NATO soldiers, machine guns in their hands, nervously looked at me, but said nothing and did nothing. They stared, either out of ignorance or surprise at what I was doing. During the war, UN forces had strict orders from the UN Security Council not to interfere in the fighting on the ground, only to escort convoys with humanitarian aid, and to fire back only if someone fired at them. When the war ended and NATO took over to keep peace in Bosnia, it kept the policy of noninterference. I wasn't yelling at them, so they perhaps assumed they didn't have to interfere.

"I know you. Your name is Meho." I spit his name at him. "You know the Heleta family. My uncle was one of your best friends before the war. Remember shooting at my home?"

The driver's window was open slightly. I knew he could hear me.

"I know the Heletas," he said, not looking at me, "but I didn't shoot at anyone during the war."

"You came to my home and took my grandfather to kill him on the bridge! Remember what you said? 'After I kill your grandpa, I'll come back for the rest of you!' After what you did to us, you think you can drive through here without getting a bullet in your head?!"

He tried to say something, but I yelled over his voice.

"I can get over starving, freezing, bleeding, losing my home and everything my family ever owned, but I can't get over what you did to us."

He finally looked at me. I saw fear in his eyes.

"The scars you made are too deep to heal."

His jaw started shaking. He placed a hand over half of his face to hide the tremors. Suddenly, he started crying. He did this before, on the day he came to murder my family.

"You cried when my grandma reminded you of how much help you received from my family. Still, that didn't stop you

from terrorizing us. I want you to be as frightened as I was when you came to my home. I want you to feel the fear I felt for so long. Your days of kicking people around are over!"

"You have mistaken me for somebody else. I . . . I didn't . . . I never did anything bad to anyone," he mumbled through tears.

In any other circumstance, I would feel pity for a grown man crying in front of me and wiping his nose and eyes with his sleeve. But not now.

"Lie to somebody else who doesn't have nightmares because of you. I'll never forget your face. That look of joy when you told us you would exterminate all of us like bugs."

Often this man had stormed into my dreams. Suddenly in a room where my family was sitting. Screaming at us. Shooting. Blood on the carpet, walls, my face, my parents, my sister.

I ran to my friends who were watching nearby.

"I need a gun right now!"

I was seventeen, no longer the little boy who had to be a victim. Now I could fight back. I didn't care about consequences. My only thought was to kill the bastard.

My friends had heard before about my experiences during the war. They told me now that they would be with me whatever I decided to do.

"I know somebody who has guns. Let's go! We'll help you," one of my friends said. He understood my rage and wanted revenge too. His father had been killed in Goražde during the war.

"The convoy won't be going anywhere for a while. They are negotiating a safe passage with the police," another friend said.

"And Meho can't run away," I added. His truck was blocked in the middle of the convoy, stopped in hostile territory.

In no time, we sought out a friend of ours who lived about two hundred yards from the place where the convoy had stopped. His father was a member of a special forces unit and their house was packed with guns. Many times when his dad wasn't around, we would go to the woods and practice shooting from handguns and machine guns. My friend's dad wasn't at home this time. Without even asking why we needed the weapons, my friend gave us a handgun and a grenade.

"I'll stand next to you, Savo. I'll protect you if the UN soldiers try to stop you," one friend said.

"I have a grenade. I'll watch your back," another one said.

I wanted justice. I felt that if I didn't take the law into my own hands, those who had tormented my family would never be punished for their crimes.

"I don't care about other people in this convoy. I just want to kill this monster."

I had the gun. I checked it. The bullet lay in the gun barrel, poised to kill. I covered the gun with the sleeve of my shirt and walked toward the truck. I wanted to have a clear shot.

1

The yard where we dribbled and shot baskets every day was filled with kids, everybody laughing and giggling and glad to be on summer vacation. Some played soccer, while younger children played with their toys in the grass. Among them was my sister, Sanja, jumping rope with friends.

Two identical three-story apartment buildings bordered the yard. My family lived in one of them. Business offices and garages enclosed the other two sides of the large space. Ours was a private, secure oasis, even though the jammed streets of downtown were just beyond the walls. The parents, at work, weren't afraid to let their children play here.

In the summer of 1990, Goražde, the city where I lived with my family, was a very safe place. People often commented that Yugoslavia was a country where anyone could fall asleep on a park bench or in the middle of a forest and nothing bad would ever happen. I spent most of my free time playing outside with friends, without parental supervision. We often stayed out until late evening hours playing hide-and-seek in

My sister Sanja
and I in 1984.

the neighborhood. At the age of ten, my friends and I often biked for miles to the suburbs or hiked the hills that surrounded the city.

Goražde is located in the eastern part of Bosnia and Herzegovina, sixty miles from the Bosnian capital of Sarajevo and the mountains where in 1984 the Winter Olympic Games were held. To get to the city, one has to pass through breathtaking canyons and drive up and down strikingly beautiful hills and mountains. Goražde sits in a wide valley, with the river Drina, its water clear blue for the most of the year, flowing through the city center.

My dad and his friends often said that, in the 1970s and 1980s, there was almost no unemployment in Goražde. Thousands of people worked in small and large companies located in the city and its surrounds. Many worked in agriculture, producing healthy organic food and supplying local markets. The climate in the region, with four distinct seasons, was great for living and farming. Like in all small cities, almost everyone knew everyone else, either personally or through other people. It seemed that they all lived intermingled in peace and harmony.

Map of Bosnia.

My father, Slavko, was a prominent journalist, reporting from the city for various newspapers, local radio, and sometimes TV Sarajevo, the main Bosnian television channel. In addition to his devotion to his family and friends, he had an exceptional love for food, which could be seen in his slightly round belly. In 1990, he decided to take a break from journalism and start a private retail business. My mother, Gordana, a

The City of Goražde in 2007.

woman with black curly hair and glasses, worked in the administration of the largest state-owned company in the city. We had a cabin in the hills, about fifteen miles west of the city, where we used to spend almost every weekend. With their salaries, my parents could afford almost anything. In the summer of 1990, we decided to start building a swimming pool next to our cabin. Dad said it would take time, maybe a few years, to completely finish it, but it would certainly be done.

In our childhood, my sister, Sanja, who was two years younger than I, and I didn't know much about issues of religion and ethnicity. Everyone in my family was a member of the Communist Party and, following the party rules, paid no attention to the church and religion. We knew about Christmas and Easter only because on those days we would have a delicious family lunch and call our friends over to enjoy cake. In 1990, on our way back from the Mediterranean Sea, we toured an Eastern Orthodox monastery. It was the first time my parents had brought my sister and me to a religious site.

One day, when Sanja was in the second grade, she came home from school and asked Mom if she could go to a local Muslim mosque to pray.

"Most of my friends from school are going. I want to go too."

"Sanja, only Muslims go to mosques to pray. You cannot go because you don't know the customs," Mom answered.

"Does that mean my friends are all Muslim? Who are we? Are we Yugoslavians?"

"Yes, we are all Yugoslavians. Our family, besides being Yugoslavian, is Serbian. Our religious tradition is Eastern Orthodox, even though we don't practice it," Mom explained.

My parents' best friends were Muslims, Serbs, Croats, and people from mixed marriages. Sanja's and my friends were a diverse lot as well. My best friend and first neighbor, Mirza, was a Muslim. We spent most of our childhood playing together. In school, we sat together at the same table. Whenever one of us got into a new sport, the other followed. We knew that he was a Muslim and I was a Serb, but in our minds and eyes, we were the same.

Being a journalist, my dad closely followed the political campaigns prior to the first multi-party elections in 1991. After more than four decades of Communist rule, all kinds of political parties emerged immediately after the breakdown of the Berlin Wall and collapse of communism in Eastern Europe. I remember my parents and their friends, who after the collapse

My dad in 1991.

Not My Turn to Die

of communism became members of the Reformist Party, which gathered people from all ethnic groups, getting irritated by the notion that everything they knew could soon crumble. After forty-five years of peace and prosperity, the new popular nationalist politicians claimed that the people in Yugoslavia—Croats, Muslims, Serbs, Slovenians, and others—couldn't co-exist anymore and had to be separated, with borders, walls, and fences between them.

The nationalist rallies were always packed. I remember one Saturday before the elections, when the Muslim national-ist party had its rally in the sports arena in Goražde. My friend Mirza and I sneaked in to see what was going on. We weren't there to listen to the politicians. We were impressed by the large crowd waving green Islamic flags with white crescents and stars, chanting in delirium when the top Muslim national-ist leader emerged on the stage. We never missed basketball and handball games played in the often-packed arena, but this time the crowd swelled like never before. Even the playing field was jam-packed with people. Many had to stay outside, listening to the political speeches on a large sound system.

After the elections, which the nationalists overwhelming-ly won, the country was in turmoil that spread like a virus. The political crisis was soon followed with the real fighting in Slovenia and Croatia, the two republics in the north that want-ed to separate from Yugoslavia. In Bosnia—home to a mix of three different ethnic groups—Muslim nationalists wanted independence from Yugoslavia, Croats wanted the territory pop-ulated with a Croatian majority to be incorporated into Croatia, and Serbs wanted to incorporate the territory with a Serbian majority into Serbia. The problem in Bosnia was that there were no clear-cut boundaries—there weren't three different regions, one for each ethnic group. People lived in ethnically mixed cities, villages, neighborhoods, and apartment buildings.

Not My Turn to Die

Tensions could be felt in my city once the fighting and violence began in the north. The media showed images of war and destruction, and many feared that the same could happen to us. In some neighborhoods checkpoints and barricades started rising overnight. My parents and our neighbors decided to start locking the main entrance doors to our apartment building. Yet the war in parts of our country seemed far away to my friends and me. We went to school every day, did our homework, and played outdoors.

One day after school, Mirza and I decided to try to build a barricade like the ones we had seen on TV. We picked the entrance to the parking lot in front of our apartment building as the location for our barricade. Big garbage cans, scraps of metal, old tires, pieces of wood and plastic—everything we could find we put on our barricade. It was big enough that no car could enter the parking lot.

Soon after we were done, residents began coming back from work. Before long, there was a lengthy line of cars idling outside the lot, their drivers waiting to park and go home. Some even got angry and shouted at us. Our parents also came back from work and realized what was going on. Our game had turned into a commuter nightmare. Very embarrassed, they made us clean up the mess we had made.

Ordinary people in Bosnia tried to prevent the escalation of ethnic violence. In many cities people organized themselves into "citizens' forums" and tried to influence those in power to find a peaceful way out of the crisis. My dad and grandpa, together with many of their friends, organized the citizens' forum in Goražde. For the most part, they were ignored by the politicians on all sides.

Well-known musicians organized concerts in almost every city in Bosnia, where thousands, both young and old, with Yugoslavian flags and messages that called for peace and tolerance, rallied to show the nationalists that they were against any kind of violence and conflict.

The biggest concert was held in Sarajevo, the Bosnian capital, in the summer of 1991. My sister and I happened to be there at that time visiting our relatives, and we decided to go to the concert with our older cousin.

We were lucky to get there a few hours before the concert began. More than thirty thousand people couldn't get in the packed sports arena. Tens of thousands of people waved Yugoslavian flags all over the place. Many prominent individuals gave short speeches, asking the nationalists to find alternatives to fighting and to preserve the peace. The best bands from Bosnia played that night.

At one moment, a group of mine workers, in uniforms and helmets, emerged on the stage. One of them held a large cardboard sign in his hands that said peace. The letters were made from red and yellow flowers.

People chanted "Yugoslavia, Yugoslavia." One of the mine workers attempted to speak, but the chanting overpowered the massive sound system.

When the crowd calmed down, the mine workers addressed the rally.

"We don't ask the politicians to change our lifestyles. We only ask them to prevent war in our country," one mine worker said.

"Look at my hands!" another mine worker said, and paused while showing his hands to the crowd. A close-up of his hands was shown on two big screens. "I work hard every day with these two hands. I go underground and dig coal so my

Not My Turn to Die

children can have food on the table and, I hope, a better future. Don't ruin our lives with your conflicts. Please save the peace!"

The vibe in the arena was electrifying but positive at the same time. People there weren't angry at anyone. They only wanted to continue with their lives, and protect their human dignity and their children's futures.

"Look at this crowd. There is no way someone can get these people to fight against each other," said a woman standing next to us. She was holding a baby in her arms.

"I've spent my life living in harmony with everyone. We went to school together. We work together," an older man added. "We never cared who was from which ethnic group. Why would we fight now?"

"The nationalists think we will follow them and fight against our friends and our neighbors. We've proved them wrong tonight," the woman with the baby said.

A man standing in front of us joined the conversation: "I voted for the nationalists, but I don't support them anymore. When they were making promises before the elections, they said we would live in prosperity and peace, better than we lived under the communists. I see now that they lied to us, that they only want to divide us."

The people left the concert full of optimism. To those who were there, it seemed that the majority were determined to save the peace.

By mid-April 1992, fighting had broken out in many parts of Bosnia. Unlike the neighboring cities, my city was still spared. Still, even without fighting, tensions were high.

People in the neighborhood talked about seeing barricades and checkpoints controlled by people with guns and black masks on their faces on all the main roads coming into the city. When I went out to play with my friends, I could see policemen now wearing blue combat uniforms, similar to those used by soldiers, and carrying machine guns in addition to handguns and batons.

With the fighting nearby, scores of refugees began arriving in Goražde. They were all Muslims, either running away from the fighting or being forced to leave their homes by Serbs. The officials estimated that the number of refugees was between thirty thousand and forty thousand. The overcrowded city housed the majority of them in primary school and high school buildings and the main sports arena in my neighborhood. People slept on sports fields and classroom floors, sharing a handful of public restrooms.

In the last days of April 1992, instead of playing soccer or other games we usually played, my friends and I wandered around the sports arena looking at the large crowds of refugees. They kept arriving in cars and buses, on open trucks and tractors. Most of those who ended up in the sports arena seemed to be people who didn't have relatives in the city or who were too poor to afford decent housing.

During one of those days, my friends and I were present at a staged fight for bread among the refugees in front of a foreign TV crew. The president of the local Red Cross in Goražde came to the sports arena accompanied by the TV crew. I realized the TV crew was foreign because two of them spoke a language I didn't understand and had a man translating for them.

"I need about thirty refugees. They should be mainly children, women, and old people," the Red Cross president authoritatively said to the refugees standing outside the sports arena.

Not My Turn to Die

When the group gathered, the Red Cross president addressed them: "You must stand around the truck transporting bread and pretend to fight one another like you haven't eaten any food for days. I don't want to see anyone smiling. You must look miserable."

They obeyed. The Red Cross was their only hope for survival.

Standing near the truck, I could clearly see and hear everything. When the TV crew signaled that they were ready to videotape, the refugees started their "fight" for food. Surrounding the truck, they began yelling and pushing one another.

"Give me some bread, I haven't eaten for days," a young man shouted in desperation, shoving women and children around him.

"I need bread to feed my kids. They are starving," a woman cried, trying to get closer to the truck.

Two men threw loaves of bread from the truck. At one point, they threw a big paper bag full of bread. The refugees, elbowing one another, ripped open the bag and fought for the loaves, which had scattered all over the place. The fight lasted for a few minutes. When a man from the TV crew signaled that the videotaping was done, the Red Cross officials calmed the refugees down and told them to disperse.

"You can keep the bread," one of the Red Cross officials shouted.

During the whole process, the TV crew looked professional and never questioned anything that was going on around them. The scene looked like someone was in the process of making a movie. When the filming was finished, everyone went on with their business just as before, as if nothing had happened.

This event baffled me for some time. I couldn't understand why someone would stage such an incident. There was enough misery in the city to film and show to the world.

By May 1992, my parents understood that it would be hard to avoid fighting in our city while there was ethnic fighting going on all over Bosnia. However, like many people my parents knew, they hoped that the fighting wouldn't last long and that reasonable people would emerge to find a way out of the crisis. My mom and dad refused to believe that people who had grown up together in peace and friendship, had gone to the same schools, spoken the same language, and listened to the same music, could overnight be blinded by ethnic hatred and start to brutally kill one another. They simply didn't accept as true that less than two years of a multiparty system and competition for power could poison people's brains so much.

We'd never made enemies. We didn't expect anyone to harm us, so we decided to stay in our home.

2

"Wake up, children. It looks like the fighting has started in the city," my mother said as she rushed into the room where my sister, Sanja, and I slept.

Still bleary-eyed and half sleeping, I heard gunshots and explosions echoing outside. It was early morning on May 4, 1992.

I jumped out of bed and ran to the window. I wanted to see if it was just like the Rambo movies.

"Get away from the window! This is not a game. Get dressed and come to the living room. The shots seem to be coming from the hills, so the living room should be the safest place in the apartment since it's on the other side," Mom said.

Sanja and I obeyed Mom's order, realizing that she was very serious. As soon as we moved to the living room, there was a terrific noise. It sounded like someone screaming outside. I'd never heard anything like it before.

"Dad, what's that?" Sanja asked.

Before he answered, a loud explosion shook our building. I heard windows crashing in the neighborhood.

"It's an artillery shell. It sounds like it exploded some-where around the police station," Dad said. The police station was just across the street from us.

For a while, one artillery shell after another exploded in our neighborhood, each preceded with the same frightening scream. Heavy gunfire echoed nearby.

My mother panicked. "We should go to the basement! I don't think we are safe here. Projectiles are exploding just across the street." Before we could respond, a large projectile, definitely larger than all the previous ones, exploded, bom-barding our building and the yard with shrapnel, metal, con-crete, and other debris. The blast was so powerful that it shat-tered one of the windows in our kitchen.

"Let's go downstairs immediately, at least to the stairway on the ground floor," my mother insisted.

We left the apartment. Our neighbors panicked too, run-ning downstairs and gathering in the main stairway on the ground floor, which had only two small windows in the corner and looked relatively safe. The adults began discussing the situation.

"Don't look through your windows. My friends phoned me and said that snipers are firing on the city," one of the neighbors said.

"We should have some chairs here in the stairway and clear some rooms in the basement so we can hide there also if projectiles start hitting our building," someone else added. The basement was used primarily as storage for wood and coal and looked too filthy for people to use without cleaning it first.

"We should also keep the main entrance door locked at all times and let in only the people we know," another person suggested.

Our parents told my friend Mirza, his sister, my sister, and me to sit in a corner that was farthest away from the windows. They said that should be the safest part of the stairway.

Sitting in the dim and crowded stairway wasn't fun. Someone brought a few chairs for older people. Most of us had to sit on the cold concrete.

After about half an hour, the shelling of our neighborhood finally ceased.

"It's quiet. I think we could go back to our apartments now. There is no point in sitting in the stairway forever. If they start firing again, we can come down," my father said.

At about eleven o'clock, our phone rang. My father answered and at the other end was his uncle, who lived in a nearby suburb.

"Slavko," Dad's uncle said, "snipers are firing on anyone who is moving. Two of your cousins were just killed by the Muslim sniper fire from the city. Milko was in front of their house when they were murdered. Stay in your apartment and don't try to get over here."

It turned out that my dad's cousins were the first two people killed on the first day of fighting in Goražde. They fell on their doorsteps, unarmed. We were shocked by the news of their death. Prior to this moment, I had seen the war only on TV, but now there was fighting on our doorstep, and the victims were people I knew. My parents wanted to go and see their families and attend their funerals, but it was too dangerous to go outside.

Who fired the first bullet? No one will ever know. Muslims will blame Serbs and Serbs will blame Muslims. Sadly for the people who only wanted to carry on with their lives, after that first bullet was fired, endless human suffering followed.

During dinner on the first day of the war, my parents had a conversation with my sister and me. Their facial expressions revealed their anxiety.

Not My Turn to Die

"The situation is very dangerous. You heard what happened to our relatives. We all have to change our behavior in order to be safe," Dad said.

"Don't go out to the balcony or stand close to the windows," Mom said. "In the evenings, don't turn on the lights. We will put sheets and blankets on the windows in one of the rooms, so we can turn on the lights there."

"How long will we have to live like that?" Sanja asked.

"I don't know. I hope not too long," Dad said.

My family lived in an apartment building in the city center on the east bank of the river Drina, across the street from the police station, sports arena, and city library. Our apartment was large and comfortable. It had two bedrooms, a living room, a kitchen, a bathroom, and a large balcony. The living room and the kitchen faced a large yard and an identical apartment building, while the bedrooms and the balcony faced a business complex. We benefited from having buildings that limited our view. While our neighbors who lived on the floor above us were totally exposed to the direct sniper fire from the hilltops, our apartment was largely hidden behind walls.

Before the fighting began, the majority of Serbs left the city and surrounded Goražde from the suburbs and hills on the east and west banks of the river Drina, fighting Muslims who positioned themselves inside the city. The distance from the place where my family lived to the closest fighting zone was only about 250 yards.

In the first days of the war, the city streets were completely deserted. People feared exposing themselves to the projectiles and sniper fire outside. After a while, people figured out risky spots and directions from where the snipers were firing on the city and through word of mouth informed one another where to be careful. The most dangerous spots were the two bridges over the river Drina in the downtown area and the street where my family lived, since the police station—one of the main targets—was located there.

The phone links to the rest of the world were cut off on the first day of the war. While the local phone lines still worked, we tried to find out who else from our family and friends had stayed in the city. Only my father's parents, Nikola and Jovanka, had stayed. They lived three blocks away, but we weren't able to see them for weeks due to the fighting. My parents phoned all their friends, discovering that many, both Muslims and Serbs, had left the city. Many of our neighbors were gone too.

<hr />

About ten days into the war, the whole city lost electricity. The Serbian forces that held the city under siege severed the main line that carried power to the city. No other source of electric power existed. Even the local phone network stopped working after the electricity went off. A few days later, Serbs closed down the water system that carried water to the city. Their strategy was to slowly force Muslims in Goražde to give up fighting by cutting off everything people needed to survive.

Everything that we had taken for granted before the war was gone in a moment.

"How are we going to live without electricity and water? How are we going to watch TV? How am I supposed to wash my hands when there is no water coming out of the pipe?" Sanja asked our parents while we sat in our dark living room.

"This is only temporary. The fighting will soon stop and they'll fix the power and water supplies," Dad said. He was still optimistic, believing that the politicians would soon stop the fighting and solve the problems at a negotiating table.

"For now, we have to start conserving water. Those plastic containers filled with water in the bathroom should last for a while. Please be as economical as possible," Mom said.

Like everyone else, we improvised for the first time in our lives in order to survive. Even though the days were becoming hot, we had to use a wood stove for cooking. We were lucky to have the stove we used for heating our home during winter months. In our basement we had some stocks of wood and coal, which we used very sparingly, to make them last as long as possible. In the first days after the electricity was cut off, we used candles for light, but our supplies were soon gone. We had to come up with an alternative or sit in the dark in the evenings. Some neighbors told us about oil lamps. We would take a small glass, fill it with cooking oil, and put a cotton string in it. Only the top of the string would stick out through a metal cover, and that part would burn and produce light like a candle. A glass of oil lasted a long time and gave enough light so we didn't have to sit in the dark, evening after evening. When the cooking oil became scarce, we used motor oil from cars. While burning, it created a dim, flickering light, a bad smell, and a lot of black smoke, but it was still better than complete darkness.

Not having running water in our home was our biggest concern. To get water for drinking, cooking, and hygiene, we had to go either to the police station across the street or to a nearby residential neighborhood called Vranjska Mahala. There, we could get clean water from wells. Every time someone went out to get water from the wells, that person risked being killed by a Serbian sniper from the surrounding hills. Running back with canisters filled with water would slow people down and make them even more vulnerable to getting hit. Even though it was very risky, and in many cases deadly, people simply had to do it.

I was so completely intrigued with running across the streets while snipers fired that I decided to ask my dad if he would take me with him to get water. In my thirteen-year-old mind, the war around me still seemed like a game. When I asked, Dad was furious.

"Are you out of your mind? It's dangerous to run across the streets."

"I know, but I would like to go with you one evening. I'm not afraid. We could get enough water for two days if I go with you. Some of our neighbors send their kids to get water," I said.

"Forget it! I don't care what other people are doing. You're not going anywhere."

But I kept asking. My parents began to worry that I might try it by myself. Finally, one quiet evening, my dad called me.

"Do you still want to go to get water? If I take you, do you promise to stop asking me to go out after tonight?"

"I promise!" At that moment I would have promised anything in order to see how it would feel to run across the street where snipers fired all the time.

We took four plastic canisters and left the apartment. Dad gave me two smaller ones, about two gallons each, while he carried two bigger ones.

It was early evening, still just light enough to see. I saw no one outside. When we approached the street, my dad stopped me.

"You go first. Run as fast as you can. When you get to the other side, hide behind that wall and wait for me," Dad said, pointing to the building on the other side of the street.

I looked around. The street and the surrounding buildings had been pierced by artillery shells and bullets. I saw that the police station had been hit by shells dozens of times. The street was littered with the scrap and rubble.

My heart started to beat fast. Up to this moment, I had thought that running across the street would be fun, but now I was scared. Still, I wasn't about to tell my dad that I was afraid. I summoned all my strength and courage to force my heavy legs to move and approach the open street.

With the empty canisters in my hands, I began running, hoping for the best. Luckily, snipers didn't fire that evening.

Inside the police station, there was an old well. Since there was no electricity, the water pumps didn't work, so we had to get the water manually. We lowered an old metal bucket attached to a rope into the well about a dozen times to fill our canisters.

After we got the water, Dad and I ran back. When we got home, my sister asked if I'd been afraid running across the street.

"Of course not! It was a piece of cake," I said, not mentioning the fear I'd felt the whole time I was outside.

We had to completely change our living habits, using water only when necessary. I couldn't even think about taking baths every day, as I had done before the war. That was really stressful in the beginning, especially because the oil lamps produced a lot of smoke and soot, most of which would end up on our faces and clothes, but after a while I got used to it. And when we washed ourselves, we could use only one bottle filled with half a gallon of water, either cold or warmed by the sunlight on our balcony.

Prior to the conflict in my city, when fighting began in Slovenia, Croatia, and other parts of Bosnia, my parents had bought some extra food in case of shortages. We had enough food for about three to four months—cooking oil, flour, rice, beans, canned meat, vegetables, and other food that needed no refrigeration. After the electricity went off, my parents threw away most of the food in the fridge and our large freezer, which had melted and started to smell bad. The same held true for our

Not My Turn to Die

neighbors. The fighting and constant artillery shell and sniper fire paralyzed the entire city. My parents, like the rest of the populace, had stopped going to work from day one. Sanja and I and the rest of the school children had stopped going to school. The city, its economy, trade, and municipal government shut down. All the food stores closed. Food that people had in their homes would have to suffice for an indefinite period of time.

Without electricity, we had to be creative and innovative in order to keep up with the news. We had a small radio that operated on batteries. For a while, we used the batteries we had. After the batteries went dead, my dad took a battery from his car and from then on we used it for listening to the news. Since the radio didn't demand a lot of power, the car battery lasted for a long time. We listened to the radio every day, hoping to hear an announcement of a peace agreement among the three sides fighting in Bosnia and Herzegovina.

Like most of our neighbors, we were very naive in the first weeks of the fighting. We still didn't truly understand that the real war was going on in our city. We thought that there would be only sporadic fighting by the extremists on both sides, not a real civil war. We hoped we could somehow stay out of it.

After we got used to the daily firings on the city, together with our neighbors, Sanja and I sometimes went out to the yard surrounded by the two three-story identical buildings, the business complex, and the garages. We thought it was relatively safe from artillery and snipers firing from the hills. The surrounding buildings gave us hope that we wouldn't be touched.

One day, while Sanja was in the yard with a friend, I heard people yelling in the distance. The voices came from the street leading to the bridge over the river Drina, less than a hundred yards from the place where we were.

Not My Turn to Die

"Don't go there. It is too dangerous. Wait for the night to come," someone near the police station yelled.

A barrage of bullets from the hills interrupted the yelling.

I stood at the window, listening to the people who ran into our yard. Among them were three policemen.

"A man wanted to go across the bridge. We told him to wait until dark. He didn't listen. He said he had to go right away. When he was in the middle of the bridge, Serbian snipers from the hills shot him in the back," a policeman explained to a group of people gathered in the yard.

"They waited for him to get to the middle. His dead body is lying on the bridge," another policeman added.

Later that day, I heard from the people in the yard that the man had apartments on both sides of the river, and apparently he'd been trying to get to his food stocks in the apartment on the other side of the river. His dead body stayed in the middle of the bridge for five days. No one wanted to risk being shot to move him and bury his body. Ironically, the man was a Serb, of the same ethnicity as those who killed him.

I often wondered how the people fighting out there could distinguish who the enemy was, especially since it had never been possible to tell apart the people from various ethnic groups in the former Yugoslavia. There was no way one could tell who was a Serb, Muslim, Slovenian, Macedonian, or Croat just by looking at that person's physical appearance. The only way to make a guess was with knowledge of someone's first and last name, but even in such cases, one could make a mistake. People could have the same last names, even the same first and last names, but be from different ethnic and religious groups.

It was May, almost summer, and the days were becoming very hot. A few days after the man was killed on the bridge, the smell of his decomposing body, exposed to the sun, became unbearable. I could smell it in our home, especially when the

Not My Turn to Die

wind blew toward us. Finally, on the fifth day, a bulletproof van used by the Muslim military forces drove across the bridge, and the people in the van used metal hooks to lift the dead body and move it from the bridge.

This van was the only way of getting across the river, since the Serbian forces located in the hills surrounding the city fired on anything and anyone moving. The van, previously used to deliver newspapers, had been redesigned to be bulletproof on all sides, except for one small hole in front left for the driver to see. I'd seen it once when it was parked overnight in our yard. Thick metal sheets covered every inch of the van.

One day the bulletproof van drove across the bridge from the west side of the river. It was a very clear shot for the Serbs who were in the hills on the east bank of the Drina, looking directly at the bridge. They fired hundreds of bullets, and one ended up going through the small hole used by the driver, killing him. We heard later that a man sitting next to the driver took the wheel and somehow drove the van across the bridge to an area not exposed to Serbian snipers and machine guns.

From the first day of the war, Goražde was under constant artillery, rocket, and sniper fire by the Serbian forces. Snipers fired on everyone moving around the city. The intensity of bombings changed from time to time, but there were not many days when at least some projectiles didn't explode in the city. The explosions were scary, but even scarier were the sounds of the shells flying and screaming through the air. One never knew where they would land.

After a while, we got used to their sounds and detonations. Even though we cleaned some rooms in the basement in the first days of the war, we used them only once, when Serbian airplanes flew over the city and bombed an area on the west side of the river. We stayed in our home for the most part,

Not My Turn to Die

going to the stairway on the first floor only when the projectiles exploded around our building.

By the noise created when a projectile was fired, we could now even recognize the difference between 60-millimeter, 90-millimeter, 120-millimeter, and bigger shells. I often hid behind the curtains in our kitchen to watch them exploding across the river and once even on the police station, only about sixty yards away. While our yard seemed to be protected from direct hits, that wasn't true for shrapnel and debris. After explosions nearby, shrapnel and pieces of concrete and metal would fly everywhere, many ending up in our yard.

Explosions in the neighborhood shattered all our windows in the first weeks of the war. Broken glass lay everywhere. We cleaned up the glass and put large, clear, plastic bags on the windows to stop the wind from blowing through the apartment.

Sanja and I, being kids of eleven and thirteen, often had brilliant childish ideas even after the fighting broke out. One day we decided to place a tape recorder powered with batteries on our balcony to record the sounds of gunfire and projectiles exploding.

Behaving like an older brother who knew what he was doing, I told Sanja, "Just imagine, almost all our friends and relatives have left the city. They'll totally miss the war. It will be cool to play them the tapes when they come back. They'll be impressed by our bravery."

"I don't know if we should do this," Sanja said. "Mom and Dad told us not to go outside. Snipers are shooting all the time. I'm afraid to go on the balcony. We can tape it from inside."

"No, the sound wouldn't be as good as if it were recorded outside. You stay in and signal to me if Mom or Dad are coming, and I'll go to the balcony with the tape recorder," I said.

Soon after we began implementing our plan, our mother entered the room. Sanja had no time to warn me. Mom called me to get back inside.

"What are you doing? Why are you out on the balcony? Didn't we tell you not to go there? You never know when a sniper could fire," Mom yelled at us.

"We wanted to record the sounds of gunfire and explosions. As soon as the war is over, all our cousins and friends will come back home and we will play them the tapes of the war they missed," I said.

"You're not allowed on the balcony anymore." She looked uneasy, worried we would go out again. "If you really want to record it, do it in the room," Mom said.

I was getting used to that look on her face. She was becoming increasingly worried about the situation and our future.

3

ay 15 began like just another war day. Explosions echoed and snipers fired on the nearby main street. My sister and I played cards with Dad in our living room, while Mom was busy preparing lunch in the kitchen.

At about 1 p.m. someone knocked on the door. Dad left his cards on the table and walked to the door. When he opened it, I saw three policemen standing outside, holding machine guns known as AK-47s.

"Hello, Slavko," said one of them, "we have a warrant to search your home for weapons, munitions, and communication devices."

The policeman handed him a warrant. My dad read it over.

"Well, I see this is official. It's signed by the police chief. You go on and do what you have to do," Dad said.

"You can't go outside or touch anything while we search your apartment!"

"I should tell you before you start that I have a legal gun with a permit and a box of bullets. If you want, I will show you where they are," my dad told them.

Legally owning a gun was quite common in the former Yugoslavia. For someone to get a gun permit, the person had to have a clear record, as my dad did. He had fired the gun only a handful of times at our cabin in the countryside, checking from time to time to ensure that the gun was still working.

"We'll have to confiscate your gun and bullets," a policeman said.

"How am I going to defend my family if someone attacks us? These are crazy times," my father said.

"We are only following orders."

My father had no choice but to give them the gun and bullets. In return, they wrote a certificate stating that the police had confiscated the gun.

After that, the police searched the apartment. They checked everything, ransacking our rooms, kitchen, bathroom, all the cabinets, looking under the beds, even going to the basement and our garage. The only place they hadn't searched was our balcony.

"If we go out to the balcony, the Serbian snipers might fire at us," the policemen said. "We will trust you when you say you have nothing illegal there."

During the same week, the police searched the homes of all the other Serbs in our neighborhood. The homes of our Muslim neighbors weren't searched.

"Why are they searching our home and not our neighbors'?" Sanja asked our parents a couple of days after the police had searched our apartment. "My friend Elma told me they never searched her home."

"Because we are Serbs and other people are Muslims," Dad said.

"But why can Muslims have weapons?" Sanja was still puzzled.

"Because they control the city and make the rules." Dad shrugged.

I was also confused by the behavior of the police. I had grown up across the street from the police station. I viewed the policemen as nice people we kids could ask for help at any time. Now they came to my home carrying their machine guns and telling me not to touch anything while they rifled through my toys and textbooks. Did they think we were criminals? Did they think my father would hide something illegal among his children's books and toys?

After the search, I could see my parents becoming more and more worried about the situation. My father wasn't as optimistic about anyone finding an alternative to bloodshed.

At the same time the police started ransacking the homes of Serbs who had stayed in Goražde, they also began breaking into the apartments and houses of those Serbs who had left the city. The policemen who broke into an apartment below ours told my parents they were looking for weapons and munitions. After breaking down the doors and rummaging through the interiors, the police would leave the apartments open for anyone to come in and take anything.

Real anarchy in the city began with the mass looting that started in the second half of May. Overnight, many people who were our neighbors and fellow citizens and had lived normal lives became looters and thieves.

We lived in the part of the city with many stores and bars, and a large shopping center. I could see from our windows the smash-and-grab spree and scores of people pillaging merchandise. They broke in and stole goods in broad daylight. Captivated by greed, many risked their lives running across the streets under the Serbian sniper fire with heavy loads of stolen goods in their hands. The police, in the station just across the street, clearly saw what was going on, especially since no one was hiding. But the police never did anything to stop the mass robbery in the very city where they were supposed to preserve law and order. In the world I lived in prior to the war, the police existed to protect the people and property and to secure safety and order. When the war began, the same officers were still in uniforms, but their job description seemed to be completely different.

I witnessed mass hysteria, people young and old pillaging everything from snacks to TVs and furniture. They behaved as if it was completely normal to break into a store and steal anything they wanted. Not long before, we'd all been customers in the same stores.

What had happened to these people? They hadn't been like that before the war. Why had they suddenly changed and become looters? How did they lose their values overnight? How did they plan to live again in organized society after the war was over?

"If you ever find a lost wallet, go to the police station and leave it there. Don't ruin someone's life by taking his or her money and spending it. Never take anything that isn't yours. You will only be happy with money and valuables you earn with your own hands." This was one of the first lessons my sister and I had received from our parents. It was repeated throughout our childhood over and over again.

After working as a journalist for more than a decade, my dad had decided to start a retail business with two friends in 1990. They had two small stores in the neighborhood and another, big store on the other side of the river Drina. They sold everything from TVs to newspapers. They had dreamed of

Not My Turn to Die

opening a chain of stores in Goražde and surrounding cities, naming the stores A, B, C, D . . . , hoping to one day use the entire alphabet. When someone asked if they planned to stop after using all thirty letters of the Serbo-Croatian alphabet, they said that they would use even the Greek alphabet if things went well.

I remember Dad coming home in the evenings after collecting the cash from the stores. He would regularly bring a bag full of money, and Sanja and I would help him count it. Dad and his friends always gave us some of the small change after counting. Usually, that was a lot of money, more than we could spend on sweets and video games. I remember one day taking half of my fourth-grade class out for Pepsis in a nearby café with the change I'd gotten the previous night.

Witnessing the mass looting in the city, Dad thought about saving his merchandise. Right away, he gave up the store across the river since it was impossible to get there safely. He tried to save some merchandise from the two stores nearby. He went to one store twice and brought home a few boxes of cigarettes, candles, and snacks. When he went there for the third time, some people had already raided the store, grabbing the products they wanted. Seeing that, Dad returned home, not wanting to get into a conflict with the looters. The other store was looted the next day. The stealing in the city lasted for about a week, until there was nothing left to steal.

The anarchy culminated when people broke into the city library, stealing books and burning them to cook food. The majority of people who did this were the refugees living in the sports arena and the primary school and high school buildings in our neighborhood.

The city library stood just across the street from us. Day after day, people carried stacks of books in their arms through

Not My Turn to Die

our yard. We couldn't believe anyone could burn these books, which had been collected over decades. Some of our neighbors protested and tried to stop the refugees, but without any success. The police, located nearby the library, saw all that was happening, but they never did anything to stop the looters.

For days, I wondered how they had the heart to burn books. Yes, the refugees were living under harsh conditions and had to somehow survive, but there were other ways of cooking food. They could have burned furniture or cut trees in parks. Because of my deep love for books and literature, it was very difficult to watch all this.

My dad, having been a journalist, had a passion for writing about events and taking notes and photos. In the first days of the war, he started writing a journal. His entries included his personal analysis of the media reports from the different sides about the war in our city and country. He also took notes of the happenings that he could see or hear about and fighting zones he could locate by the sounds of gunfire and explosions. He planned to write about it once the war was over and give his personal account of the war in our city. He took photos from our windows of the projectiles exploding and buildings burning.

After the police searched our apartment, my parents constantly worried about keeping the journal and photos.

"If they consider us spies and search for communication devices in our home, what would happen if they discovered your journal?" my mother asked my dad. "They would arrest you right away."

"I hoped they wouldn't find the journal all the time they were here," Dad said.

"You better stop writing and taking pictures."

Without a word, Dad walked to my parents' room, took the camera from his cabinet, and pulled out the film. From one

Not My Turn to Die

of his folders he pulled out a notebook, and then brought everything to the kitchen.

"It hurts to do this, but these are crazy times. I hope something will remain in my memory if I ever decide to write about the war," he said, burning the film and his journal entries in the wood stove.

"I was outside yesterday when I saw five policemen escorting a Serbian man to the police station. I can't remember his name, but I know he lives in an apartment attached to the primary school building and is a teacher," a Muslim friend told us in the first week of June 1992.

"That's my physical education teacher. What happened to him?" I asked.

"The policemen pushed him with their guns, his hands handcuffed behind his back. Who knows what they did to him," our friend explained.

The next day, the whole neighborhood talked about the teacher's arrest. Almost everyone knew him, since he lived only 150 yards away from us. I heard people in the yard saying that the police apparently had found a two-way radio transmitter and a sniper rifle in his home. They considered him a spy for the Serbian side. Some of our neighbors even loudly claimed that every single Serb who remained in the city was a clandestine agent, the so-called fifth column, and should end up arrested like my teacher.

We soon heard that my teacher had been taken to a newly formed prison in a residential suburb across the river. A few days later a story went around that he was killed there and his body thrown into the river Drina.

In my home, the story about my teacher's end frightened us. He was arrested and killed perhaps by those same policemen who had ransacked our home searching for weapons. Did he have a gun or did they just say that so they could justify killing him? *What will happen to us?* we wondered. What would happen if they really consider us to be the fifth column? And what do they really mean by the fifth column? My parents tried to explain it to my sister and me, saying that the term was used to describe people whose goal is to act in a subversive way by supporting another side in the conflict.

"When they say that we're the fifth column, they think that we're helping the Serbian side. They think that we stayed in the city to be spies," Mom said.

"We don't have anything to do with the war. We just live where we've lived all our lives. We're not harming anyone," I protested.

"Not many people use their brains anymore. They just blindly follow the lead of the politicians who created all this mess," Dad said.

The arrest and death of my teacher was only a precursor to more arrests and killings in the city. By the end of the same week, my grandfather visited us for the first time since the war began and told us about arrests in his neighborhood. A Muslim man who had recently moved into my uncle's empty apartment had told him he'd seen the police arresting all the Serbian males, more than ten people, in my uncle's building. Among those who were arrested was a man named Todor, our close family friend. He was one of the kindest and friendliest people I have ever known. To make things worse, he wasn't even Serbian. Instead, he was a Bulgarian, married to a Serbian woman. His first name, Todor, is very common among both Serbs and Bulgarians. The Muslim police arrested him and others without asking any questions. A day after their arrest, the wife of one of the men arrested visited my grandparents and in tears told them about the previous day, when the police had taken her husband and son away.

After they were taken to the same prison where my teacher was killed, one of my grandfather's Muslim friends recognized Todor there. He told Grandpa that he'd seen him and other Serbs in front of a house, near the banks of the river Drina. They were all tied to a fence with wires and ropes, their heads and clothes covered in blood, facing the sun. After being tortured, they were killed and their bodies were thrown into the river.

Not one of those arrested was ever seen alive again. They were accused of spying for the Serbian side, supposedly sending flashlight signals from the city to the hills where the Serbian forces held their positions, and having weapons and two-way radio transmitters. None of them ever had a criminal trial. The mere accusations were enough for the death penalty.

Somehow, my family was spared in the first wave of killings. We experienced only the ransacking of our home and feared daily for our lives under heavy bombings and sniper fire. Yet, we feared that things could get only worse in the future. Without a way out of the city, we could only hope the fighting would end soon.

4

"Don't fool with us. We know you've stayed in the city to spy for the chetniks!"

Smelling of homemade plum brandy, a man named Rasim weaved back and forth in his chair as he accused my parents of vicious crimes. "You are all the same to us! Some of you kill us with artillery shells and snipers, and some of you kill us by sending information to your friends. We know you radio the chetniks with our military positions. And your neighbors told us they saw you sending flashlight signals to the hills."

It was June 17. We'd heard from our Muslim neighbors that Rasim had burned down a number of Serbian houses in the area since the fighting started. A drunkard with a scarred face and a penchant for picking fights, he was someone my father would never have let into our home before the war. No rational person would trust him. Yet, the Muslim police had recruited him once the war began.

My parents didn't want to let him in. His machine gun changed their minds.

He interrogated my parents for more than four hours; my sister and I remained silent and still between our mom and dad on the couch. Dressed in a green camouflage uniform, Rasim sat on a chair, smoking one cigarette after another. His machine gun rested near him on the dining room table, the gun barrel pointed toward us. I watched his hand move toward the AK-47 whenever an answer didn't satisfy him. Fondling the barrel, sliding his finger toward the trigger.

The spy and flashlight stories weren't new to us. My teacher, our friend Todor, and many others were accused of being spies and killed without a trial. The killers could never find evidence, and in our case the flashlight accusation defied logic. Buildings surrounded us.

"The police were here once and they searched the whole apartment," my father said. "They didn't find anything illegal. I had a gun procured with a permit and some bullets. They confiscated them and gave me a certificate."

My mother almost shouted, "The police can come again and search our home if they suspect we are still hiding something."

Rasim ignored them, "Better you admit guilt now, rather than later. I know people who are ready to take you to the river. A bullet in the head, they roll you into the Drina, and then you float all the way to Serbia."

My parents looked at each other, then at my sister and me. I could see they were frightened. They said nothing.

Rasim sat for a moment waiting. Abruptly he brandished his gun and said, "If you don't cooperate, the river will be your grave." Then he got up and left, slamming the door behind him.

We sat frozen. Terror seized me; bloodcurdling thoughts spun around my mind. We could only wait for death! Our only hope was for a quick death without much pain.

My father broke the long silence. "Did you hear what he said? They consider us to be chetniks. How absurd!"

Chetniks had made up the Serbian nationalist army in World War II. They fought against the Nazis, communists, and Croatian and Muslim pro-Nazi forces. Like other sides in the war, they had committed many crimes against civilians, particularly Muslims, Croats, and Serbs dubbed communist sympathizers. My extended family had been partisans, the communist guerrilla forces, fighting to liberate the country and its people from the Nazis and the local nationalists. They had fought against chetniks, and here, decades after World War II, people dared to brand *us* chetniks!

***

The next morning at about six, the sound of someone breaking the building's entrance door downstairs awakened me. Sanja and I slept in one bedroom, our parents in the room next to ours.

I shut my eyes tightly and decided I was having a bad dream. Thuds on the door downstairs and yelling from the people breaking in proved me wrong.

They broke the main building door downstairs and ran up the stairs, shouting obscenities. Within seconds, they kicked at our door with their heavy boots and bashed it with their shoulders.

"Open the door, you bloody Serbs. This is your last day!"

My little sister cried my name in fright. She jumped from her bed and started dressing. I jumped from my bed too and rushed through my stuff on a chair, looking for pants and a shirt.

"Open the door! We know you are in there!"

Our room door was open. I saw my mother, frantically trying to dress in the hallway. She asked them to wait, not to break down the door.

"Open right now or I'll blast it open with my machine gun. We don't have time for games. Too many of you chetniks live around here. This will be a busy day for us!"

I heard them cock their guns.

"Whatever happens, please don't leave your room," Mom pleaded with tears in her eyes. She hugged Sanja and me before closing our bedroom door.

"No!" I flung the door open. "We want to be together." I looked at my parents and sister, thinking that it could be the last moment we would see one another alive.

There was no time for discussion. My mother opened the main door and asked what was going on. No answers, just yelling. Four men with guns in their hands and long knives and hand grenades hanging on their belts cursed and took aim at my mother: "You dirty chetnik, this is your last day."

Four monsters with haggard faces, hatred pouring from their bloodshot eyes, and reeking of brandy, screamed, "Bastards! Chetniks! Animals!" They made one promise: They would exterminate us once and for all.

"We're going to kill you like dogs!" one of them yelled over and over and over again.

My mother knew him very well. A man named Suljo. She and he had been neighbors in their youth and had grown up together. A short, bald man in his late thirties, he had worked for the municipal government before the war. The faces of the other two men, in their early twenties, looked familiar to me. I'd seen them many times in the yard before the war. They had friends living in our building. I remembered the nickname of one of them. Celo. The fourth man didn't look familiar.

One of them grabbed my dad by the collar and dragged him

out to the stairway. Another one did the same to my mom. She held out my father's leather jacket, trying to give it to him.

"Drop it or I'll kill you! She has a grenade in the jacket!"

"It is only a jacket. . . ." Her voice was trembling. "See, nothing in the pockets."

One man snatched the jacket from my mother and searched it. "Your husband won't need the jacket. After today, he won't be able to wear it again." Checking the size of the jacket, he said, "Look, guys, nice leather. It's my size."

Then he looked at Sanja and me. He seemed confused to see children.

"Kids, get out of the apartment and follow your parents," he finally yelled. When Sanja and I started to slowly walk outside, he shoved me with his gun barrel, almost knocking me on the floor.

"Please don't hurt the children," my mother pleaded with them. "Do whatever you want to us. Just don't take the children."

"Shut up. You won't tell us what to do. You Serbs, you are no good! You are nothing!" one of the intruders said, laughing madly in my mother's face.

In the stairway, our Muslim neighbors Adem and Amra, parents of my best friend Mirza, appeared at their doorway. They'd awakened after hearing the racket coming from our apartment. They wanted to find out what was going on and where the four men were taking my family.

"Go back to your apartment and don't ask any more questions, or else you could get hurt too," one of the intruders said.

Adem and Amra didn't retreat. "Please, at least don't take the kids with you. Leave them here with us," Amra begged.

The four men stopped. The intruder named Suljo took another man aside, talking to him for several seconds.

"Okay, the kids can stay with you for a while. That will make our job easier," Suljo said.

"When we are done with their parents and the other Serbs from the neighborhood, we will come back for them. They'd better be here," another man added.

My sister and I didn't want to stay with our neighbors. We cried until our throats were raw; we wanted to stay with our parents. If we had to die, we wanted to die together. Our neighbors pulled and pushed until the two of us were safely inside their apartment.

Adem and Amra tried to calm us down. They assured us that somehow everything would be fine, that our parents would come back unhurt. But Sanja and I could hear the four men wildly yelling at our parents in the stairway, calling them chetniks and Serbian spies.

Suddenly, gunshots rang out. Utter despair engulfed my heart. I was out of my mind, crying like never before in my life.

This is it, I thought. *They have murdered my parents.* The very parents who had raised me to respect everyone, who had provided me with everything I'd ever wanted. My mom and dad, who had loved me so much, had now been killed.

My sister and I broke down, begging our neighbors to let us go outside to see what had happened to our parents. Our neighbor Amra wept too, pleading with us to stay with them. Her husband hid the key to the main door to keep us inside.

I was hysterical. I just wanted to find my parents' bodies, but they wouldn't let me go out. They moved me and my sister into the living room.

In shock, Sanja and I sat in our neighbors' living room, sobbing more quietly now. The noise coming from the stairway downstairs ceased. Suddenly, our neighbor Adem ran from the kitchen to tell us that he'd just seen the four men taking our parents and another woman toward the city library and the primary school. Upon hearing this miraculous news, Sanja and I started laughing.

"They are alive? They didn't die? What about those gun-shots?" Sanja asked, wiping tears away from her face with the sleeves of her shirt.

I ran to the kitchen to see with my own eyes that they were alive. I looked through the window but couldn't see anyone.

"Where are they? I don't see anyone. Didn't you just say that you saw them? How could they disappear all of a sudden?" I asked. I wanted proof they were alive. I had to see them with my own eyes. I thought my neighbor had lied to me to calm me down.

"I swear I saw them," Adem said bluntly. "They must be behind the library by now."

Silently, I stared out the window, yearning to catch a glimpse of my parents. Nobody was outside. All I saw were deserted streets, buildings, the river, and the fog that hid the surrounding hills. The city seemed eerily calm.

I suddenly remembered the threats from the previous day, when the man named Rasim had promised that my family would be killed and our bodies thrown into the river. Adem said he saw them going toward the city library and my primary school. That was right by the river.

I told our neighbors what Rasim had told us the day before. After that, Sanja and I began crying again. In a state of absolute despair, we sat on a couch and wept in anguish. Our neighbors tried to comfort us, but there was not much they could say.

Sanja and I were at our neighbors' place for about an hour when someone knocked on their door. My first thought was that the four thugs had come back for us. Yet, this knocking was polite, not like the banging on the door by heavy boots earlier.

"Who is there?" Adem asked.

"It's me, Nikola, Slavko's father. I'm looking for them."

Sanja and I looked at each other. Our grandpa was here. We wanted to run out to the hallway, but our neighbor told his wife that he had to talk to him first. To prepare him for the news.

The living room door was slightly open, and I could hear their conversation in the hallway.

"Nikola, please come in. Sanja and Savo are here. Gordana and Slavko were taken by four men with guns not long ago."

Grandpa opened the door and entered the room. He was holding a small plastic bag in his hands. His face looked like he wanted to say something, but I could not hear anything. I only saw his jaw shaking.

He came to sit next to us and began crying, covering his eyes with his hands. I couldn't see his face now, only his snowy white hair. My grandfather used to be a member of the parliament of Bosnia and Herzegovina, the city mayor in the 1970s, and later the top manager of one of the big companies in the city. In my eyes he was the most powerful man in the world. This was the first time I'd ever seen him cry.

Seeing him shed tears made me even more frightened. I'd always thought he could fix any problem easily. Now he was sitting on the couch next to me, looking helpless and destroyed.

Grandpa put the plastic bag on the small table in front of us. "Your grandma baked cookies for you. That's why I came this morning." These were the first words I'd heard from him since he appeared at our neighbors' door.

Sanja and I looked at the cookies at the table. We were in no mood to eat.

Adem and Amra explained in detail what had happened and how the four men wanted to take us with them also. Still in shock and not fully understanding the situation, I commented that the four thugs had said that they'd be back for us once they had killed our parents and other people.

This news was just too much for Grandpa. He jumped from the couch and dabbed tears from his eyes. "You are good people, and I thank you for saving Savo and Sanja, but they cannot remain here. Those monsters will come back, take them away, and kill them," Grandpa said in a shaky voice.

"Where are you going to take them?" the neighbors asked.

Grandpa shrugged. "I don't know. All I know is that they cannot stay in this building any longer."

He told Sanja and me to go back to our apartment and quickly pack some clothes. We were to go with him to his home. There we would decide what our next move would be.

Sanja and I ran across to our home to pack.

After seeing the anarchy in the city, I figured our home would soon be raided and we'd lose everything. *When we leave, people will break in as they did to all other empty apartments and take anything they want,* I thought. I told Sanja that we should try to save some food. She nodded and began opening the cupboards.

We decided to hide flour, beans, rice, canned food, and other stuff behind beds, couches, and shelves, in the washing machine, even in the big fireplace in our room, as if it would be safe there.

There were no tears and there was no discussion. We were just two kids with an impulse to survive. When our grandfather came to our apartment to get us to go, we weren't ready. He said we must hurry up.

Not My Turn to Die

Quickly, we packed our school backpacks with food, clothes, and photos of the two of us with our parents. Sanja packed her Barbie. I filled my pockets with packs of chewing gum from the boxes Dad had brought home from his store.

Outside, the fog had reduced visibility and helped us to safely run across the city streets. When Sanja and I arrived with our grandpa at his home, our grandma, Jovanka, was happy to see us; this was the first time since the beginning of the war. But her mood changed quickly after she saw our sad faces. She sensed that something had gone terribly wrong.

When she heard what had happened, she fainted with shock. She'd lived her whole life for her three sons and their families. Now one son and daughter-in-law had been taken away and perhaps were already killed. She simply couldn't endure it. We had to give her water and sugar to revive her. She was in such shock that she couldn't even cry. She just sat on a couch and stared at the floor. At one point, Grandma stood up, insisting on going outside and looking for my parents. We had a hard time consoling her and keeping her in the apartment. She kept asking where our parents had been taken and if they were alive. She had had heart problems and had been on medications for years. I was afraid her heart might just break.

I spent the whole day in misery and despair. The images of the four thugs grabbing my parents and pushing my sister and me with their guns were embedded in my mind. I couldn't cry anymore, and that made me feel bad. *My parents are dead,* I thought, *and I can't even cry for them.*

A few of my grandparents' neighbors came to visit and talk to us. They all said that everything would be fine. They said my parents would come home unhurt. I didn't believe them. *I've heard about all those Serbs who were recently taken away and never seen alive again,* I thought. *Now the same is happening to my parents. I will never see them again. I am thir-teen, but I know what happened. I better understand that, I thought, instead of listening to these people who want to comfort me with their tales of "everything will be fine."*

It was dark outside when someone knocked at the door of my grandparents' home.

Grandpa turned on a small flashlight and opened the door. He pointed the light at the person standing outside. It was our neighbor Adem.

"Nikola, I have great news. Slavko and Gordana are alive and well!" Adem announced with a broad smile on his face.

"What are you saying? Are you sure?" my grandpa asked.

"Did you see them?" I asked as I ran into the hallway from the living room. I didn't know if I should believe him. *He's probably trying to console us like all those neighbors earlier today.* I had seen those monsters taking my parents away, pushing them downstairs with their gun barrels. I'd heard gunshots. They were taken toward the river Drina. I was afraid to hope they were alive.

"Did you personally see them?" I repeated.

"Yes, I was with them all evening. I just walked with them to the home of their friend Nedim. Savo and Sanja, pick up your stuff and come with me. You will stay with your parents there for a while."

"I too would like to go and see Slavko and Gordana," my grandfather said.

"We'll have to be careful not to be recognized by anyone. If you have hats, put them on your heads," Adem told us.

Grandma Jovanka.   Grandpa Nikola.

I was guardedly excited and happy because of a lingering fear arising from all that had happened during the day that I would go to Nedim's place and my parents wouldn't be there.

Grabbing our stuff in a hurry, I completely forgot to take the chewing gum. Sanja forgot her Barbie.

My grandfather came with us, while Grandma Jovanka stayed at home. The day had been too much for her. She too had trouble believing it.

I couldn't believe my eyes. When Nedim opened the door, holding a burning candle in his hand, my mother and father stood in the hallway.

They both started crying. Grandpa, Sanja, and I also cried. Mom, then Dad, hugged us. Then Grandpa hugged both of them.

I was afraid I could be dreaming. *What if I wake up and find myself in Grandpa's apartment, without my parents around? What if they are really dead?*

Not My Turn to Die

We moved to the small living room. In silence, we wiped away tears and looked at one another.

I longed to know what had happened to them, how they'd survived. "So, what happened to you after they took you away, after we separated?" I asked.

Taken downstairs from our apartment, my parents had been forced by the thugs to sit on the chairs in the stairway that we used to sit on when taking shelter from bombings. While two of the men tried to break into the apartment of our neighbor Slobodanka, who was also a Serb, the other pair aimed their guns at my parents' heads. They continued yelling at them, asking them to admit being spies, and threatening again and again to kill them.

Recognizing the voices of my parents in the stairway, Slobodanka worried that if she stayed inside she would end up in the hands of the men who had captured my mom and dad. She jumped over her balcony, since it was on the first floor, and ran away. Barefoot and in her pajamas, she fled her home, not knowing where go to look for help. The only people she could think of were some friends working at the city hospital.

When they couldn't open Slobodanka's door, Suljo, my mom's former neighbor, forced my mother, with the gun barrel pointed to her head, to get closer to the door and call out Slobodanka's name.

"Where is Slobodanka? Speak up or I will kill you!" he yelled.

"I don't know. She lives her own life. She doesn't tell me where she goes," my mother answered.

"Don't try to fool me," Suljo said. "I know you are together in this. You all stayed in the city to help our enemy."

My mother prayed that Slobodanka wasn't there. At gunpoint, she called out her name a couple of times.

"Louder, call her louder!"

When no one answered, Suljo pushed my mother aside and fired on the door with his machine gun. Then, he and one of his compatriots broke the door and entered the apartment. Nobody was inside.

Before they left our building, two of the thugs abducted a Serbian girl who lived in another part of our building. They locked her elderly mother inside the apartment, saying that they would be back for her and my sister and me later during the day. They forced their three captives, with their hands on their heads, to walk toward the city library.

On the way, the four men with their captives stopped in front of the home of yet another Serbian family, living behind the library. Breaking down the entry door with their boots, they dragged out a Serbian woman and left her elderly parents for later. One of them went into the house and stole coffee, sugar, and cigarettes.

Instead of forcing them toward the river Drina, the tormenters decided to take their captives to Vranjska Mahala, the residential suburb located not far away from our home. There, they forced the captives into an abandoned house. In the meantime, three more Serbs who lived nearby were brought in.

In the house, the captives were told that if one bullet or one projectile happened to be fired on the city, they would be killed immediately. Two captors controlled a living room where all the people were held, while another two oversaw an interrogation room in another part of the house. There, my parents and other Serbs were taken one by one and cross-examined.

My mother was questioned first by her former neighbor.

"Do you know that my mother was killed by Serbs only a week ago? Right now, dogs are eating her limbs on the city streets. And my wife, she was raped and killed by chetniks."

"I'm sorry to hear that," said my mom.

"Do you know who killed her? Our friends with whom we used to play in the yard when we were kids! They are now Serbian terrorists."

"Once again, I'm sorry for your mother and your wife, but what do I have to do with that?"

"You are all the same—you and those who killed my wife and my mother. You stayed in the city to spy for them. That is why you are all going to die today," he yelled.

My mother said that during the interrogation, she didn't want to cry or beg for her life. She expected to die and didn't want the thugs to enjoy her cries for mercy. She prayed and hoped to die quickly, without being physically abused and tortured.

While my father was interrogated, one of the thugs told him their plan for the day. They intended to capture all the Serbian civilians in the area and keep them in Vranjska Mahala to be used as human shields against the Serbian forces. This was possible because Vranjska Mahala was partially in the fighting zone near a Serbian-controlled suburb east of the city center. They also planned to inform the Serbian forces over a two-way radio that, if they didn't stop firing on the city, the group would execute all the Serbs they held captive.

After more than two hours of interrogation and verbal torture in that house, the main door flew open and a man named Hasan, a former police inspector in Goražde and now one of the organizers of the city's defense in the area, appeared. He knew my father and the rest of my family very well. My mom said he held a handgun in his hand and was wearing a military uniform. Pointing his gun at the two captors in the living room, he angrily yelled at them and called them idiots. He insisted that they would be severely punished for what they had done.

The captors seemed to know him and fear his authority, immediately putting their machine guns down. He told them

57

that they should go and fight the Serbian forces instead of terrorizing innocent people who had no means to protect themselves. He confiscated their guns and moved to hit one of them in the head with his fist. All the captured Serbs, except for my father, who was still in another room, stood up to defend the man who only a minute before had threatened to kill them all.

Hasan apologized repeatedly, telling the captured people they were free to go home. My mother told him that my dad was still being interrogated by two other men in another room. He burst into the room, attacking these two as well.

"You idiots, I should just kill you now!" He was furious, now holding a machine gun he had taken from one of the captors minutes earlier in his hands.

Again, it was the captives who had to calm him down.

He turned to my dad, who was still sitting in the interrogation chair. "Slavko, from this moment you are not obligated to answer any more questions. You are free to go home."

"Please don't enforce any sanctions against these men," my father whispered to Hasan so no one could hear. "We don't want them to come back and terrorize us again."

My dad's and other people's reasoning was that the penalty these men could receive would be, at most, a few days to a month in jail. What would happen after that? Who would defend us from their acts of revenge? The police certainly wouldn't, as they hadn't that morning.

My parents asked Hasan to accompany them home, which he did. He was a good and honest man, and couldn't find enough words to apologize for everything that had happened. He told my dad that somewhere in Vranjska Mahala, as my parents and other hostages marched with their hands on their heads behind machine-gun-toting oppressors, a fifteen-year-old boy had seen what was happening and informed him. Had the boy not seen what was going on, had he not cared that some innocent people were in grave danger, had he not bothered to seek out the former police inspector, all of us would certainly have died. One young person had tipped the balance for all of us from death to life. Another good human being had prevented gruesome murders.

———

My parents continued their story: When our neighbor Slobodanka escaped from her apartment and ran to the city hospital, she informed as many people as she knew that my parents had been taken hostage. One of those people was Nedim, the man in whose home we were now. He is a great friend of my father and our family. The two of them had gone to primary and high school together and continued to be friends afterward.

After my parents' release from their captors, Nedim came to see how they were doing. He helped my parents fix the main door of our apartment, which had been almost entirely broken by the intruders. The marks from the thugs' military boots were all over the door.

Mom and Dad were upset when they didn't find us in our apartment or at our neighbors' but were relieved to hear we were with Grandpa.

Our neighbors told my parents that some of the residents of our building had already come up with a story that the four men had come to search our apartment that morning and found a two-way radio transmitter and two machine guns—the reasons to murder my family. My parents couldn't understand some of our neighbors' abrupt malevolence. How could they be so callous, turn a blind eye, and even lie when criminals broke in to kill us in cold blood? We had never said a bad word to any of them.

My parents and Nedim went back to our apartment. Gathered in the living room, they discussed what to do next. Sitting on a couch, my mother felt something hard beneath the cushions. She reached in between two cushions and found a can of tuna. They looked around and found even more cans, beans, rice, and other food. They were totally confused, knowing that nothing had been there before. It was the food my sister and I had hidden. They suspected that we had this brilliant idea to hide the food, and that put smiles on their faces, the first smiles of the day.

Suddenly someone in the yard called out my father's name. Nedim told my parents to stay inside and went out to see what was going on. A short, bald man in his late forties, called Kula, stood in the yard. There were rumors that he was one of the people the police sent around to intimidate Serbs in the city. He was wearing a military uniform, holding a machine gun, and had a big knife hanging from his belt.

Kula was angry when he saw Nedim instead of my dad.

"I was never so scared in my life," Nedim jumped in to explain. "This man yelled that he didn't call me and asked why I was helping and defending Serbs. He then took out his knife and put it on my neck. I thought I was going to die right there."

My parents said they watched this in disbelief from the window of our apartment, hiding behind the curtains.

"I'll slaughter you for helping them," Kula yelled.

"They are not in their apartment. I came to look for them, and their neighbors told me that they have already left," Nedim told him.

"Don't lie to me."

"You can go and see that no one is in their home," Nedim said, hoping Kula wouldn't decide to go.

Luckily, Kula believed no one was in the apartment. He pulled the knife away from Nedim's neck.

Not My Turn to Die

"I hate Serbs, but even more than Serbs, I hate Muslims who help Serbs. If you ever try to help them, I will kill you and your family," Kula screamed.

Nedim started walking Kula away from the yard and toward the police station. While arguing on the street with Kula, Nedim saw the police chief, Mustafic, standing at the door of the police station. Nedim told the police chief that Kula had almost stabbed him. Instead of helping, the chief screamed at Nedim not to defend Serbs. Chief Mustafic told him to mind his own business if he wanted to survive.

Distressed, Nedim returned to our apartment.

"There is no way you can stay in your home any longer," Nedim told my parents. "This bastard almost killed me, and the police chief said I shouldn't be helping you if I want to stay alive. No one can protect you here."

"But where else can we go?" my mother asked.

"Be ready to leave in the evening. I'll come back and take you to my home," Nedim said before he left our apartment.

Knowing that we would be out of our apartment for an indefinite time period, my dad suggested to my mother that they find someone to move in for a while. If our apartment had stayed empty for only a couple of days, my parents thought, all we had owned would certainly have been stolen and someone would have simply usurped our home.

"We should ask our neighbors if Adem's sister would like to move in with her family," my mother said.

"They might agree since it's eight of them living in a two-bedroom apartment," my dad said.

My parents went across and talked to our neighbors. Adem's sister and her family, who were refugees, agreed to move in. They promised to take care of our possessions as if they were their own.

Near nightfall, Nedim and our neighbor Adem escorted my parents to Nedim's home. Afraid of arousing suspicions, they didn't bring a lot of belongings, only a small bag of clothes and food. After that, Adem went to my grandparents' home and brought us the great news.

In the safety of Nedim's home, looking at my parents as they told us their story, only then did I realize how close I had been to losing them. I was happy, sad, worried, and uncertain at the same time. Yes, I was happy that all of us were alive and together, but also afraid of what might be coming.

5

"Your stay here is a secret. Even our next-door neighbors cannot know you're here, only a handful of people whom we can trust will know your whereabouts," Nedim said the morning after my family had moved to his place.

"I hope no one saw us coming last night," my mother said.

"It was dark when we got here, and we didn't encounter anybody on the city streets or in the stairway of the building. I don't think anyone saw us," Nedim said.

"We will keep our voices low so no one hears us," my father said.

"Whenever you hear voices in the stairway, please go to the bedroom and hide," Nedim's wife, Jasna, said.

Nedim and Jasna lived in a small two-bedroom apartment, too small for six people, but they accepted my family with open arms. They even moved out of their bedroom so that my family could hide and sleep there. The two of them slept on a couch in the living room.

Nedim, Jasna, and a few other people who knew about our hiding catered to all our needs for water and food, often risking their own lives to procure it. Nedim went out twice a day to get water for us at a nearby well. He had to run across the streets under constant sniper fire, carrying heavy canisters with water in his hands. One time he came home with one canister half empty. When we asked him why he hadn't filled the canister, he showed us a hole on one of the water canisters where a sniper bullet went through when he was running, barely missing his legs.

Not having a stove in their home, Jasna cooked food in a neighbor's apartment. Every day, she had to find excuses for the pair's greatly increased appetites, never divulging that she was actually cooking for six of us.

The neighborhood where Nedim and Jasna lived—right next to the city hospital—had been under constant sniper and artillery fire since the beginning of the war. When shells exploded in the yard or on the building, my family couldn't go downstairs to the basement like everyone else, but had to stay in the apartment. Often, when projectiles hit the building, the apartment would shake like an earthquake had hit, with debris and shrapnel scattering everywhere. We would lie on the bedroom floor and hope to be spared.

On our third day in hiding, I was alone in the bedroom when I heard people screaming in the yard after a sniper shootout and a few explosions nearby. Curious, I lifted the blanket that covered the windows and peeked outside. On the road, not more than thirty yards away, a man carted another man in a wheelbarrow, heading toward the hospital. The man in the wheelbarrow was critically wounded, completely covered in blood. His legs were detached from his body. Screaming in pain, he clutched his legs in his arms.

I moved away from the window and sat on the bed, frozen in fear. I couldn't believe my eyes. I had never seen anything like this. I sat petrified, the scene I'd just witnessed swirling in my head.

The horrendous image of the man holding onto his detached legs haunted me and stayed embedded in my mind for days. My dreams became full of blood and destruction. I was in no mood to eat or talk to anyone. I was so weary of seeing the suffering everywhere around me, experiencing oppression, my family hiding in the small room, the poor man without legs—none of it made any sense to me. I kept asking myself why all this was happening to my family. Why was this happening in my country? Why were people so crazy?

With every passing day, I sank deeper and deeper into despair. I stopped talking, laughing, playing cards with my sister and chess with my dad. I vegetated. My days felt very long, but I didn't care. I didn't care about anything anymore.

One day I entered the bedroom and found a little religious calendar on the small table by the bed. My mom had looked at the dates of some religious holidays and left it there. There is a belief among Serbs, even those who are not religious, that people shouldn't do any serious work during religious holidays and on Sundays.

I looked at the calendar and found the Lord's Prayer and some other prayers on the back. After a long time, I was finally interested in something. I decided to try praying to God. If there is a God, I thought, it might hear my prayers and help my family in these dreadful times.

I didn't know anything about God or religion. I only once in my life had entered a church. I never seriously talked about religion to anyone. I only remembered seeing my great-grandma making a sign of the cross and praying quietly when I was still in kindergarten. I decided to try making the same sign of the cross countless times every day after saying the Lord's Prayer, asking God to give my family, at least, just another day without fear and war. My mother noticed this one day, but she didn't say anything. I also saw her doing the same.

It was almost July, already three months since the war had begun. My sister's hair was getting too long, covering her eyes. I was ready for a haircut too. One day, Dad decided to cut our hair using small paper scissors.

"I've never cut anybody's hair, but it shouldn't be hard. Let's cut Savo's hair first."

I explained how I wanted him to cut it, as I had always done before the war when I went to hair salons. But my dad didn't know what he was doing.

After about ten minutes Dad announced, "Look in the mirror and see what I did. Exactly as you wanted."

I looked in the mirror. Not only was it completely different from what I wanted, but it looked terrible. The hair length was totally uneven, especially on my forehead. I complained, but my parents, Nedim, and Jasna persuaded me that my hair was just fine.

Then it was my sister's turn. She only wanted to shorten the curls on her forehead. Unfortunately, Sanja's haircut also looked horrible, even worse than mine. She lost her curls on her forehead, and more than half the length of her hair. Sanja almost cried when she saw herself in the mirror.

"Don't worry; no one will see you. Your hair will grow back," my mother said.

We all stared at one another in silence. Mom was right. We didn't have to worry about our hairstyles or how we looked or dressed. We were fugitives in our own city, lucky to still be alive.

Whenever we heard voices in the building stairway, my parents, sister, and I hid behind a large bed in the bedroom, behind the door, or, in the case of Sanja, even in a closet. Whenever someone knocked on the door, I always feared that the thugs had found our hiding place and had come to kill us. In each of those frightening moments, my pain became physical as well—a gnawing pain in my stomach making me keenly aware of the fear that dominated my life.

One evening, when someone unexpectedly knocked on the door, we moved to the bedroom and, behind the closed door, remained motionless and mute. We didn't dare to make any noise that could lead to our exposure.

Jasna opened the entrance door and started talking to someone. We listened, tense.

"Hi. How are you?"

"Good. My husband and I were in the neighborhood visiting a relative who was wounded recently and decided to stop by," a woman said.

"Come in for a coffee," Jasna said.

The woman and her husband were Nedim and Jasna's friends. They didn't and couldn't know about our hiding. For more than two hours, we stayed in the bedroom. After a while, my sister became antsy.

"Mom, I need to go to the bathroom," Sanja whispered in distress.

"We have to wait until they leave. They can't find out we are here."

"I've waited for so long. I don't know how much longer I can wait."

Sanja nervously bit her nails. I felt bad seeing her suffer, hoping that the people who visited would be leaving soon.

After a while, the living room door opened and I heard Nedim and Jasna saying good-bye to the visitors.

Sanja's face showed a pained expression, but she smiled after hearing the entrance door opening and the guests leaving.

As soon as they were gone, Nedim opened the bedroom door.

"Are you okay?"

"No!" shouted Sanja and ran to the toilet.

"What's wrong with her?" Nedim asked.

"She really has to use the bathroom," I explained.

"I'm sorry, but this was the first time they visited us since the war began. We couldn't tell them to leave," Nedim said.

From time to time, some of our Muslim friends, a handful of those whom we trusted, would visit us at Nedim and Jasna's home and give us moral support to endure our hardships. They usually arrived in the evenings or at night, when there weren't many people around to observe their comings and goings. It all had to be done in total secrecy.

These visitors told us the stories circulating in the city regarding my family's disappearance. One said that we were killed on June 18, and our bodies sent to the Serbian side, after which they were seen floating in the river Drina. Another rumor was that we'd escaped from the city and that my parents had already been seen fighting against the Muslim forces. Yet another said that we were still hiding somewhere in the city.

Some of these visitors were in high positions in the Muslim army. They told us that the army hadn't been responsible for the organized killings of Serbs in the city but the city mayor and his government and the local police forces had. We learned from them that Serbs murdered in the previous months never had access to a lawyer or a trial. About a month after they were killed, the city mayor ordered one of the judges in Goražde to write death sentences with forged dates to have documentation in case of possible future investigations.

One friend, a high-ranking military officer, told us about a meeting of the top Muslim military and civilian representatives at which he was present.

"One of the topics at the meeting had been the ongoing arrests and killings of Serbs in the city," he said. "Myself and a few other military officials openly disagreed with the mayor, Hadzic, who wanted to liquidate every single Serbian civilian that stayed in the city. Fighting against those who are attacking you is noble, but torturing and killing innocent people is simply unacceptable for us. After some harsh words, one of our top military commanders took out his gun, put it on the table, and said to Hadzic that if any more Serbs were tortured and killed by the police, without first being found guilty, he would hold the mayor responsible and personally kill him."

"What did the mayor say after that?" my dad asked.

"Nothing; he left the meeting angry. He said we were all traitors for defending Serbs."

Hearing the stories of organized terror perpetuated by the city mayor and the police and fearing that the situation could only deteriorate further, my parents asked our friends if they could help us cross the dividing zone between the Muslim and Serbian forces to escape from Goražde.

"This is not our war," my father told them. "We stayed in the city because we never did anything bad to anyone. Now I see that in a war, you don't have to be guilty in order to be terrorized and killed. We just want to leave."

"We will leave behind all we have," my mother said, "if we can only get out of the city. We must go far, far away from this place."

"It is too risky to undertake such an escape," one of our friends said. "If you, Slavko and Gordana, were alone, we would try it, but we cannot risk the lives of your children."

My parents understood their reluctance. If we attempted to escape, we would have to go somewhere into the woods beyond the city, stay in a Muslim trench, and wait for an opportune moment to run across to the Serbian side. Serbs wouldn't know our identities or purpose, so there would be a strong chance that they would kill us on the spot. We had heard that a few Serbian civilians had died this way when they'd tried to escape from Goražde.

For days, we lived without seeing sunlight or breathing fresh air. The windows in the bedroom, covered with blankets, didn't admit any daylight. A painting on the wall of the bedroom where we spent almost all our days was in such shadow that I never even became aware of its detail.

I began feeling claustrophobic in the small, dark bedroom. The walls seemed to be closing in on me. It felt as if there wasn't enough room even to turn around. I missed open fields, running around, playing with friends, having fun. I felt like a caged animal.

"Dad, how long do we have to live like this?" I asked one night.

"I don't know. We can't go back to our apartment. The people who attacked us are free. They could come back to kill us at any time."

"I'm not sure how long I can stay in this small room. It's so claustrophobic."

"We all feel that way, Savo. Please be strong. There is nothing we can do now, but stay here and hide. If we go out, we risk being killed," my father said.

I had to be strong. My parents and sister were in the same position, and they didn't complain, at least not out loud. I knew that Mom and Dad worried a lot but tried not to show it in front of Sanja and me. I decided to keep my feelings to myself.

One evening, we all sat in the dark living room. Using candles was prohibited on that side of the building, even if the windows were covered with blankets, since it directly faced the hills west of the city from where Serbs fired. If they saw any light, they would immediately send sniper and cannon fire toward the building.

The night was quiet, and we chatted before going to bed. My dad and Nedim smoked a cigarette together. It had been two weeks since my dad decided to gradually quit smoking. From a pack, he got down to three cigarettes a day. Nedim, on the other hand, smoked as heavily as always, even when he had to mix tobacco with tea leaves to make his cigarettes last longer.

Suddenly, a deafening blast threw all of us to the floor from the chairs and couches.

My ears felt numb. All I heard was ringing.

At first, I thought Nedim's apartment had been hit by a projectile. It was dark and I wondered if I was alive.

"Is everybody okay?" I asked. "Is everybody okay? Answer, please!"

The room was quiet.

"I'm okay," Sanja finally said.

"What happened?" my mother asked.

"A projectile exploded somewhere really close. I hope no one is hurt," Jasna said.

After a moment, someone started screaming on the next-door balcony. I completely froze. I'd never heard anything so disturbing. It was a cry of agony and horror.

I heard a child asking, "Dad, what happened? Why are you screaming?"

Plastic bags, used to replace windows that had shattered long before, had been ripped apart in the explosion, so I could easily hear people talking next door.

"Don't come over here," a man wept. "Please don't come to the balcony. Go to the basement and stay there."

"I should go and see what happened," Nedim said and left the apartment.

The man next door continued wailing in grief: "Why . . . why did this happen? God, why do you have to be so cruel?"

I heard other people trying to calm him down.

"She said she needed some fresh air . . . she could not stand being inside all the time. That's why she stood on the balcony," the man tried to explain.

Nedim soon came back, his voice trembling. "What a horrific scene!"

"Did someone die there?" my father asked.

"Our neighbor was killed on the balcony. It's . . . her body . . . it is totally torn apart. Her husband and kids are unhurt. They were inside when the projectile exploded. I will go back there to see if I can help clean up."

We stayed in the apartment, even though there was fear of more projectiles. We couldn't go to the basement like the rest of the residents, whom I could hear panicking and running down the stairs. We had to stay in and hide. We moved to the bedroom, where we could barely hear the cries of the man who had just lost his wife.

My grandparents couldn't come to see us in our hideout even though they lived only a block away. The only time my grandfather visited us was when he came to make sure my parents were alive after being taken hostage. We feared that the police or the thugs who wanted us killed would connect my grandparents' visit with us and would come to search Nedim's apartment.

Grandpa Nikola heard the rumors that some people were, in fact, beginning to suspect that Nedim was hiding us. He'd heard this from some of his Muslim neighbors and sent a message by one of them to my father. This prompted my parents to have a discussion with my sister and me.

"What Nedim and Jasna are doing is noble, but we shouldn't stay here anymore. If our tormentors find us here, they may not only kill us, but also everyone who is helping us," my mother said.

"I agree. We should go somewhere else. But where?" my father said.

We didn't have many options. We could either go back to our apartment or move in with my father's parents. In the end, we decided to move to my grandparents' home. In the building where they lived, Serbian civilians had not yet been attacked,

Not My Turn to Die

nor had anyone been taken away. In contrast, in a building just across the street, all Serbian males had been taken away by the police and killed.

Nedim and our Muslim friends urged us not to go. They tried to persuade my parents to stay longer at Nedim's place or to hide somewhere else, but not to go out in the open.

"We can't put you or anyone else in danger anymore. If they find us here, they might harm all of you for helping us," my father said.

In all the horror that surrounded my family, there was some goodness too—the proof that nothing in the world could break a true friendship. Some of our Muslim friends risked being marked as traitors of their own people by helping the "enemy." They could have justified turning away and ignoring us, as many others did. But no! They put their lives on the line to save ours.

After twenty-two days in hiding, we waited for night to come, and walked over to my grandparents' home. As we stepped outside, it felt so good to be able to breathe fresh air again, to see the sky, the moon, and the stars.

The night was quiet. A crisp breeze filled my lungs with fresh air that for weeks I longed for. For a moment, it seemed like a peaceful summer night in Goražde before the war.

The moon gave us some light to travel by. As soon as we approached the main street, we stopped to get ready to run across. Here was where, as our friends had told us, we were in the greatest danger of being hit by snipers using night vision.

My mother ran across the street first. Sanja and I followed, then my father. No one fired on us.

I remembered the big yard in front of the building. I'd played there with other kids whenever I visited my grandparents. Once an appealing park, it now had debris everywhere from explosions. With almost every step, I felt concrete and shattered glass under my feet. I could barely see, but I did realize that all the trees in the yard were gone. Perhaps people had to cut them down to use the wood for cooking.

Finally we arrived at my grandparents' home. They were very happy to see us again. That evening was the first time my grandma had seen her son and daughter-in-law in more than two months. It had been twenty-two days since she'd seen and hugged her grandchildren. She hadn't seen her other two sons and their families for an even longer period, but she hoped that they were somewhere safe, far away from the war.

We sat in the dark living room and for a few hours talked about the events that happened to us and them. They said that, apart from the ransacking of their home by the police, they hadn't had any other problems so far.

"From the day when those men took you away," Grandma said to my parents, "I've spent every day waiting in fear that someone would come and bring news that something bad had happened again. At least we are all together now. I hope our suffering will be over soon."

6

I was in a deep sleep when, at about two o'clock in the morning, banging at the door awakened me. Sanja and I had been sleeping on the floor in the hallway of our grandparents' home ever since we'd left Nedim and Jasna's home a week before. Our parents considered the hallway the safest place in the apartment, since it had no windows facing the hilltops from where guns and cannons fired on the city.

"Nikola, my name is Inspector Hokic," I heard a husky male voice outside say. "I order you to open the door. I have a police warrant to escort you to a center for isolation." By this time, we'd heard many stories about this Inspector Hokic. People said he had been in charge of arresting most of those Serbian civilians who were never seen alive again.

Grandpa's neighbor who lived in the apartment below, was also on the other side of the door. The police had ordered him to talk to my grandpa, to persuade him to let the police in.

"Nikola," a neighbor called, "please open the door. There is no reason for fear. The police are here."

Upon hearing loud banging on the door, we were all up in a second. We were already dressed. We now slept in our clothes, with shoes by our beds and mattresses, ready to run down to the basement in the middle of the night in case of bombings or if someone came looking for us.

Dad and Grandpa told us to stay in the living room. Dad lit an oil lamp and took it with him. Grandpa had no other choice but to open the door. If he didn't open it, they would probably have broken it in. That was their specialty. They had practiced it on hundreds of abandoned Serbian homes when they conducted their searches.

Five policemen entered the apartment. They said we should all gather in the living room. A man who again repeated that his name was Inspector Hokic handed the warrant to my grandfather. He was a tall man, in a police uniform, with an AK-47 in his hands.

The warrant stated that we were to be taken to a "center for isolation" for Serbian civilians, located in a building in Mose Pijade Street. The building was right next to the building where my family had lived, just across the street from the police station.

"You have fifteen minutes to get ready. Bring food and clothes for three days. You won't need more," Inspector Hokic told us.

"What's going to happen to us after three days?" Grandpa asked.

"I'm not authorized to talk about that. You'll find out when the time comes," Hokic replied.

After hearing this, I lost the last bit of hope for survival. They weren't going to set us free in the midst of a war. Telling us that we needed food for no more than three days meant to me only one thing: certain death.

Bleary-eyed after waking up so abruptly, shocked, and confused, we packed in a hurry and in silence. We grabbed random things since there was no light to see except for one little oil lamp.

Before we left the apartment, Inspector Hokic read a statement signed by the city mayor, saying that they were going to put us in a "center for isolation" to protect us from Muslim extremists and to prevent us from collaborating with the Serbian forces that kept the city under siege.

We went outside into the dark yard. Some people, holding little plastic bags in their hands, already waited there. Many policemen surrounded us, pointing their machine guns at us.

When they had gathered all Serbs from the neighborhood —about twenty people—we were told to start moving. The police led us between the buildings and through dark alleys that seemed even darker and more horrific with them pointing their guns at us and shouting to move faster.

I remembered this neighborhood from the time when my friends and I would sneak in and steal fruit from the gardens. Our parents always bought us all the fruit we ever wanted, but it was a game sneaking into the nearby gardens and stealing apples, grapes, plums, and cherries. The fruits we harvested ourselves always seemed to taste sweeter.

When we finally reached the police station building, the police told us to run across the street that was under constant sniper fire. It wasn't safe to walk across even at night, since the Serbian forces shooting at the city often used snipers with night vision. This time they didn't fire a shot.

The police ushered us into a three-story apartment building. We were told to go to apartments on the second and third floors, all owned by Serbian families who had left the city prior to the war. They randomly decided who was going where.

My family, grandparents, and two other men who lived in my grandparents' building, men named Mitar and Dragan, were placed in a room in an apartment on the third floor. Mitar was a director of a company that had run a hotel, bars, and taverns in the city before the war. Dragan was a well-known fine arts painter. Their families had left the city before the fighting began.

Eight of us were crammed in the room, about twenty by twenty feet, the size of the room my sister and I had shared in our home. We sat in the dark room, some on the beds, others on the floor, talking about what had happened to us. The future looked uncertain and dark.

I heard Sanja asking Mom, "Why did the police arrest us? Why did they bring us here? Why can't we go home?" Mom didn't answer any of the questions. She couldn't speak. She was sobbing in the corner of the room.

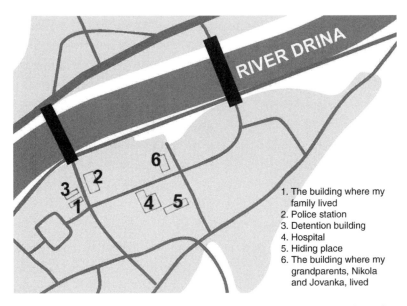

1. The building where my family lived
2. Police station
3. Detention building
4. Hospital
5. Hiding place
6. The building where my grandparents, Nikola and Jovanka, lived

Map of downtown Goražde showing the places featured in the book.

Not My Turn to Die

"What are they going to do with us?" asked my grandma. "They said we would be here for three days. Where are they taking us then?"

No one in the room had an answer.

"Please, Mom, don't panic. Don't add to an already tense situation," my dad said.

"I'm afraid they'll kill us all. God, the children are here with us. If only they were somewhere safe," Grandma whispered.

It was late, perhaps four in the morning. I could still hear police bringing in more people and telling them where to go from the stairway. I closed my eyes and tried to sleep but couldn't. So much was on my mind. I just sat quietly on the floor, thinking about what was going to happen to us.

At dawn, I glanced around the room. There were two beds, a small dining table, two chairs, and a cabinet. I realized that the apartment had been ransacked. Clothes, family pictures, and books lay in piles in the middle of the room. All the windows had been broken, and shattered glass was everywhere. We began moving things around and cleaning the room of glass and wreckage. This was where we would have to stay for now. A few days, as the police had said.

The room where we found ourselves was on the top floor of the building, facing the east and the hills from where the Serbian forces fired mortars on the city. Nothing could protect us from being directly hit by rockets and bullets.

On the second day in detention, the Muslim police chief, Mustafic, relayed the rules of conduct, which were read to us by one of his officers. The officer entered every apartment and

Not My Turn to Die

read the rules out loud. They stated that we couldn't leave the apartments or try to communicate with people outside. No food would be provided to us. The police were in the stairway on the first floor to prevent anyone from entering or leaving the building. They patrolled the stairway on the second and third floor to prevent us from communicating with one another.

Every evening at about six, a police patrol came to our rooms and counted us to make sure we were all there. We had to stand up and gather in a corner of the room that didn't face the windows for the roll call. They would point a bright flashlight into our faces for a moment.

When the neighborhood was heavily bombed on the third day and projectiles and rockets exploded around the building, my grandfather left the room to ask the policemen on duty to allow us to take shelter in the basement.

"I know it's against the rules, but it's dangerous to stay in the rooms. Shrapnel is flying around. I have two grandchildren here and there are probably more children in other apartments. Could we go to the basement?"

After short consultations among three policemen, one of them said, "We can't let you stay in the rooms to get massacred. Go and tell the others that they can go to the basement."

Grandpa came back and told us to go to the basement. On the way downstairs, he informed people in other apartments that they could go and hide in the basement.

The basement was dark and dirty. Like in the building where my family lived, this basement was used primarily for storing wood and coal for winter heating.

I sat on a piece of cardboard in one corner and could see the silhouettes of people coming in. I counted more than fifty.

My dad went around and talked to people. He discovered that his cousin was here with her eight-year-old daughter.

Detention building with bullet holes and a rocket hole.

There were two children a few years older than me. A pregnant lady, and the rest of the people were adults, most of them old.

We realized that almost all Serbs, seventy-six people in total, who had remained on the east bank of the river Drina had been arrested and brought here. Only a handful of Serbian families, those who had family members too ill to move, had been left in their homes under house arrest.

There were approximately nineteen people in each apartment, sharing one toilet with no running water. Seventy-six people used a single wood stove for cooking what little food they had. We didn't have firewood. We burned wood furniture.

One of the policemen on duty told my dad that, at the same time we were arrested, a synchronized action took place on the west bank of the river Drina. Serbs who lived in that part of the city were also arrested and taken to a similar detention building.

Of approximately ten thousand Serbs living in Goražde before the war, now only a few hundred remained, the unlucky ones who stayed. The ones with bad reasoning. At the same time, the Muslim population increased after the arrival of refugees, from about twenty-six thousand to more than fifty thousand, according to the Muslim media.

When the cannonade ceased, we went back to our rooms. Passing by the officers on duty, people thanked them for letting us hide in the basement.

Later that day, two policemen entered our room and told us to get out into the stairway. I saw that the policemen who had been on duty earlier weren't there.

"Listen carefully!" one of the policemen yelled. "Our chief sent a message saying that if you try to go to the basement one more time, he will personally come to tie you up to the fence on the balconies facing the Serbian forces, so you get killed by your people."

Somehow, the police chief had found out that we were allowed to take shelter in the basement and reacted angrily.

"From now on, you will do only what Chief Mustafic tells you to do," another policeman added. "Otherwise, as the chief said, you will regret the day you were born!"

We now stayed in our rooms even when artillery shells exploded around the building. We could do nothing but lie on the floor and hope to be spared.

This is when we realized that the "center for isolation" where "we would be protected from Muslim extremists," as we had heard in the mayor's letter on the night of our arrest, was a joke. We were prisoners in a dreadful unofficial prison. One of the policemen who let us go to the basement and who knew my dad whispered to him that we would be held in a real prison if it already weren't full of Serbian civilians who were arrested in their villages on the outskirts of the city.

The police called the place a "center for isolation." We called it a variety of names: "detention center," "concentration camp," and "ghetto." Whatever the term, this was becoming by far the most awful place in my life. A real hell on earth.

The three days that we were told we would spend in detention passed. We had brought four plastic bags of food with us. Dragan and Mitar had brought some too. We decided to put all our supplies together and share. The food was almost gone now, even though we had eaten little each day. A few plastic bags of food for eight people didn't go far.

In the first few days in detention, we ate two small meals a day. Upon realizing that the food would soon disappear, we cut down to one small meal a day. I don't know how we functioned as human beings. On some days we ate a half a potato per person. On others, we had a piece of bread and a bit of jam. And on some days we ate nothing.

I began dreaming about food: meat and potato or cheese pie, roasted lamb, steak, my mom's cakes, apples, oranges, chocolates. Waking up was hard. I would then realize that all that food on the table was only in my dream. In reality, our table was empty.

After a week of hunger and desperation, my grandfather again approached the guards, telling them that he and other Serbs wanted to talk to the local Red Cross officials about providing us with some food. One of the guards delivered the message to the president of the local Red Cross. This was the same man I'd seen staging a fight for bread among the refugees before the war began in the city.

A few days later the Red Cross president came to visit us, bringing a letter signed by the city mayor, Hadzic. He read the letter aloud in our room, in front of the eight of us and a few other people: "The food and water are provided by the police and the local government. Serbs in the center for isolation need no further help from the Red Cross."

He passed the letter around. There was a municipality letterhead on the top and the mayor's signature at the bottom of the letter.

But there was no food.

"We have known each other for many years," my grandfather told the Red Cross president. "You are the highest-ranking Red Cross official in the city and should do your job independently. Why do you obey inhumane political orders?"

"The mayor claims in his letter that you are provided with food and water. What else am I supposed to do?"

"You are here and can see that we don't have any food. Isn't that enough for you to realize that we need help? Do you

Not My Turn to Die

still believe your mayor's claims after seeing seventy-six people who are starving to death?" someone asked.

"The rules of war demand provision of food and water for people held in custody. We are not provided with any. Even Nazis provided some food, however miserable it was, in their horrific camps during World War II," my dad angrily added.

"I can't help you. I have the strict order from the mayor not to interfere. You have to influence him somehow if you want me to help you," the Red Cross president said, concluding the meeting.

The Red Cross, our last hope, had left us to starve.

To get drinking water, we had to go to the well located inside the police station. A schedule was set up by our captors that dictated when people from different apartments could go to the well. One night it would be the people from the two apartments on the second floor, and another night the people placed on the third floor of the building. Only one person from each room could go. That person, carrying two canisters, was permitted to go only once that night.

Whatever water we could get for the eight of us in our room was barely enough to drink, especially since it was summer and the days were quite hot. We couldn't even think about taking baths or washing our clothes.

We expected to soon be killed or to die from hunger under the rule of Police Chief Mustafic. He had already orchestrated the arrests and killings of many Serbian civilians prior to our arrest. Why would we expect to live?

He never showed up at the building where we were held. I never saw his face. I only heard about him, imagining him in my mind as a devil. When he was angry about the policemen letting us go to the basement to save our lives, Chief Mustafic didn't come himself to threaten to tie us to the fences. Instead, he sent other policemen to deliver the message.

Not My Turn to Die

After about ten days in detention, a large guided projectile, as the police told us later, hit the police station. It went through a window and two walls and exploded in a room where Chief Mustafic was hiding. Seriously wounded, he couldn't get help in the hospital in Goražde and had to be taken to Sarajevo, over mountains controlled by Serbs. People said he survived, but he never came back to Goražde.

Into his position came a man my dad knew very well. They were of the same generation and had gone to the same high school. As soon as he took over the control of the police station, he and his new deputy visited us.

"While I am the police chief, you won't be terrorized and will be able to go to the basement whenever there is a bombing near the building. You will also be allowed to freely communicate between apartments," the new police chief said.

He ordered the policemen to stop the routine of counting us and even allowed our Muslim friends to come and visit us from time to time. When the new police chief saw the old and sick people, he called for a doctor to come and examine everyone and bring some medicine. He said he had strict orders from the mayor and had to keep us in detention, but his behavior and humane approach helped us greatly. We felt that he, at least, wouldn't be as brutal and cruel as his predecessor.

Still, there was no food.

A few packs of cigarettes my dad had with him saved our lives. Cigarettes became worth more than gold and diamonds in war-torn Goražde. One pack of twenty cigarettes was worth around a hundred German marks or fifty U.S. dollars. Now that our friends could visit us, my father would give them a few cigarettes, asking them to exchange them for any food they could find. Realizing the value of the cigarettes, my father completely stopped smoking. He saved the cigarettes so he could put some food on the table.

Not My Turn to Die

One of our Muslim neighbors visited us once and said he would bring us extra drinking water once or twice a week. My dad promised to give him a cigarette each time. He always insisted that he wasn't helping us in order to get a cigarette in return, but he always took one. When the cigarettes were gone, he never offered to bring us water again.

One day my sister's friend Elma came to visit her. She had lived in our apartment building. Elma was eight, two years younger than Sanja. She spent the first months of the war in a village near Goražde, staying at her grandparents' house. Now she was back.

As soon as she arrived, Elma came to see my sister. She told the policemen that she wanted to see a friend and they let her in. The two of them met in the stairway.

"Hi, Sanja," Elma said. "How are you?"

"Good," Sanja answered, not looking her in the eyes. Sanja was a bit embarrassed to meet her friend in the conditions in which we lived.

"My mother told me you were here."

"Yes, we're here now. I don't know how long we'll have to stay."

This was the extent of their conversation, as they had not seen each other for months. Both of them were confused and didn't know what to talk about.

Elma had brought a present for my sister, a bag of candy. Before the war, a bag of candy was a small gift. Now, in our eyes, this was the greatest gift we'd ever received.

For the first time in months Sanja had a happy smile on her face. She opened the candy and began to give everyone a piece.

"Don't give it to us," Mom said. "Keep it for you and Savo."

"I want you all to have a piece. Savo and I can have the rest. Please take it."

It was a lemon-flavored hard candy. It tasted better than any sweets we had ever had. Sanja and I had a piece of candy every day for a few days.

Sanja and I had never been spoiled in our childhood. We never cried to our parents when we wanted something. We were happy with what we had and didn't use their kindness to get all the things we wanted. Having been raised like that helped us tremendously in these times of scarcity and hunger. We understood what was happening in the city and that there were people who wanted us dead. We also understood that we didn't have a lot of food. In many instances we were hungry for days. Countless times we went to bed with empty stomachs. Still, we never asked for more food than our parents gave us. When they tried to put more food on our plates, we always refused. We knew they would give us anything in the world if they were able to do so. My sister and I knew how much it hurt our parents that they weren't giving us enough food or a normal childhood. We couldn't add to their suffering by showing we were hungry. We kept our feelings inside and hoped that better times would soon come.

One day a man called Kenan visited the place where we were held to see some of the people he knew, including my father. He came to our room and talked to my parents for a while. He said it was a disgrace to see us living in such conditions. He asked us if the police were providing us with food. We told him the truth.

Not My Turn to Die

Before he left, my dad asked if Kenan could do us a favor.

"Kenan, please, could you find my friend Nedim and tell him that the gift of any food would mean a lot to us?"

"Yes, I'll go right away. I'm sorry to see you here. I hope this mess will end soon."

That same evening, Kenan came back and gave us a bag of food. He was in a hurry and didn't say from whom it came. We assumed it was from our friend Nedim.

When Nedim visited us two weeks later, my father thanked him for the food.

"No, the food wasn't from me. It was from Kenan. He couldn't find me and he brought you the food from his own home," Nedim said. The city officials, finding that Nedim had given us shelter in his home, had forced him to go and dig trenches in the fighting zones outside the city. Kenan had decided to get us some food on his own. He went home and packed a bag full of food, taking it away from his three children.

My father and Kenan weren't friends. They just knew each other from the city. Kenan was a bartender at a restaurant where my dad and his friends liked to go before the war. Yet he helped us with food when we were starving, showing us that there were still good people around who wouldn't let other human beings suffer or die from hunger.

We had a real feast one day. Some people brought us two wild pigs they had killed. The only reason we got the meat was because most Muslims don't eat pork due to religious reasons. It was a big day for all seventy-six of us. It was a big day also for more than thirty Serbs captured in their village, about three miles east of Goražde, and held in cells in the police station. The new police chief visited the detention building and told my parents and other people that, if there was any extra meat from the two pigs, they could prepare a meal for the prisoners and take it to them. All the elders decided to cook a big meal for everyone and these thirty people in jail, dividing the rest of the meat into equal parts among us.

Once the food was cooked, the police told us that someone had to take it to the prisoners at the police station. My mother and two other women decided to go. They needed help carrying the food. I asked if I could go with them. As there were no other volunteers, my mother said I could go with them.

With two policemen escorting us, we ran across the street with pots in our hands. It was a quiet day. Snipers didn't fire at us.

I had to carefully pick my way to the police station. The area was covered with debris, shrapnel, metal, glass, and bricks from the police building, which had dozens of holes and craters. Other buildings were destroyed too, but the police station looked like a prime target in the neighborhood.

There were no doors at the entrance. Projectiles had blown them up.

The policemen took us through dark hallways and into the jail area. Two guards opened a heavy door, and we entered a small yard surrounded by cells and high walls. The guards told us we were strictly prohibited from talking about politics or war with the prisoners.

As soon as we entered the yard, I saw people looking at us through the bars on the doors. One of the guards unlocked the cells, and people started coming out.

About thirty people came out. They were mostly old people, men and women, all thin and dirty, in old and torn clothes. Two women recognized my mother. They said they used to work for the same company before the war. Mom couldn't recognize them.

When they saw the pots of food we brought in, the prisoners started smiling and crying at the same time.

"Is that for us? Thank you so much. May God give you all

Not My Turn to Die

the best and help you and your families," an old lady repeated while crying and kissing our cheeks.

"This will be our first real meal after more than a month," another woman whispered. "May God save you and your families! May you have your freedom again! I'll pray for you every day until I die."

The guards stood quietly in corners, with machine guns in their hands.

We stayed with the prisoners for about ten minutes, until they emptied the pots so we could take them back with us. On the way back, I thought that we were actually lucky compared to them. Our living conditions, however bad, were much better than what these poor people were going through.

There was a street dog that lived in the stairway of our detention building. The dog didn't have a name, so we called her Kuja, which in Serbian means "female dog." Kuja belonged to a man also detained with us. He had owned one of the most popular bars in the city prior to the war.

He told us that "every morning when I would come to the bar, I would eat breakfast there. Sometimes I would give this dog a piece of my food. I felt bad for her when she became pregnant, so I started buying her whatever I would buy for myself. Soon, she waited for me in front of the bar every morning. I even told my employees to buy her some food whenever I didn't come in."

She wasn't a nice-looking dog. In fact, if you saw Kuja walking down the street, you would certainly stay away. You wouldn't think about calling her or touching her. Even when

Not My Turn to Die

she wasn't dirty, she looked as if she was because her fur was a grayish color.

Somehow, Kuja, who was expecting puppies again at this time, was able to sense whenever there was to be a bombing around our building. If she was outside, she would get nervous and bark in a frenzy until the policemen on duty opened the door. She would run into the building and hide in a corner or under a chair, howling. Every time she did that, there were explosions around the building within a minute. After a while we realized what she was trying to tell us, warning everyone in the building to get to the stairway or the basement.

One morning in August, Kuja barked loudly outside. We knew something was going to happen. Soon, the Serbian forces fired incendiary rockets and bullets, setting many buildings in the neighborhood on fire. In no time, fire leaped and spread onto the sports arena and the business complex right next to the place my family had once called home. Clouds of smoke covered the horizon.

I watched from our room. The Muslim refugees who lived in the sports arena ran about in fear. Here was the second home they had lost within a couple of months. From our room, I could see our neighbors standing in the yard, terrified that the flames could easily sweep over onto their homes, not more than twenty yards from the burning business complex. They could do nothing but sit outside and wait. The city's fire brigade hadn't functioned since the war began. Even if the fire-fighters had come, they wouldn't have been able to help, since the Serbian snipers fired on anyone moving around. The sports arena and the business complex burned for two days.

A few days later, on a quiet evening, we were all in our rooms. Kuja didn't show up at the door, so no one had reason to fear. All of a sudden, projectiles started exploding around us.

The apartment and the furniture shook. People in the next-door apartment began screaming and calling for help.

Did Kuja try to get the policemen's attention? I wondered as soon as I heard the explosions. Maybe they hadn't heard her.

My Grandma screamed and jumped to run out. We all scrambled for the door. My grandparents exited first, then my sister, father, mother, Mitar, and me. Behind me was Dragan.

I reached the hallway when a projectile exploded in our room. The air pressure caused by the detonation pushed me forward. I looked back and saw Dragan on the floor.

"Someone help me; I can't walk. I'm wounded."

The projectile had exploded when he was at the door. Shrapnel had hit his right leg.

"Someone come back. Dragan is wounded," I screamed.

My father and Mitar returned and dragged him into the stairway.

A frightened old woman from another apartment screamed that people were wounded there too. She was calling back to her husband, but he didn't come to the door. Projectiles continued to explode on and around the building.

Some people entered the next-door apartment, looking for the wounded. They came out carrying an old man, completely covered in blood. I could see a wound on his neck. Every time he breathed, he sprayed blood.

Screams also came from the two apartments downstairs.

"Go to the basement and see if your sister is safe," my mother told me.

"They need help here," I answered, wanting to stay.

"Go downstairs! We don't want you to be here, risking your life and seeing people bleeding and dying," my father said.

I went to the basement against my will. I would rather have stayed and tried to help, but I obeyed my parents' request.

Escorted by the police, my dad and others took the wounded people to the hospital. The wounded received help there, and returned when the cannonade ceased, later that night.

We discovered that many projectiles had hit the building, three of them exploding in the rooms. The first one wounded two old people in the next-door apartment. Another projectile hit an apartment downstairs, under our room, where two men were wounded. Among them was my primary school teacher, who died shortly afterward. The third projectile exploded in our room and wounded Dragan.

We slept that night on chairs in the stairway. The next morning, we went back to the room to clean up. Dragan's blood was all over the carpet. The projectile had gone through the balcony door and exploded in the room. We stared at the mess that the shrapnel had created. The balcony door was ripped apart and the walls and furniture had countless holes. We wanted to do something to make the room safer. The only thing we could do was to move the large wooden cabinet from the wall and cover the windows with it. It wouldn't save us if another projectile hit, but we felt safer, less exposed.

A couple of days later, some people who came to visit their friends detained with us brought bad news about Kuja. They said they had seen Kuja and her puppies killed on a street three days before. A projectile had exploded right next to them.

The people in the building were sad. Kuja had saved our lives many times but couldn't save the lives of her puppies or her own. If she had been alive, she might have prevented the massacre that wounded Dragan and killed my teacher. Some of us cried for the street dog.

The shelling of Goražde was often totally random, with projectiles exploding on and around schools, the city hospital, and people's houses and apartments. The Serbian snipers often shot at everyone—women, children, and old people—even though they were located on the hilltops not far from the city center and could probably distinguish between civilians and soldiers. I saw with my own eyes old women getting shot while scurrying across the street with water canisters in their hands.

In many instances, the shooting on the city was a response to Muslim provocations. The Muslim forces often positioned their guns and snipers on the city's apartment buildings, using them as launching pads for attacks on Serbs. I watched soldiers hiding behind the garages in the yard and firing their machine guns at Serbs surrounding the city. Often, Serbs would quickly locate them and send down dozens of projectiles and salvos of gunfire.

Innocent people were paying the price. Not one side in the war ever cared about the civilian victims. Sometimes, civilians were called collateral damage, and in other instances they were victims of revenge. There were also sadistic monsters on all sides who enjoyed torturing and killing people. Bosnia was a circle of death and terror. Not one side was strong enough to win the war, and no one was ready to surrender.

The first United Nations Refugee Agency (UNHCR) convoy with food and medical aid arrived in Goražde in the beginning of August. The trucks delivered medical aid to the city hospital. Food was stored in abandoned shops attached to the building where we were detained.

When I saw the UN soldiers with their blue helmets walking around their trucks and vehicles on the parking lot in front of our detention building, I hoped they would somehow find out about us and come to our rescue. They were so close to us, but we couldn't contact them. On this day, extra police guards had been deployed to prevent us from communicating with the UN soldiers in any way.

The quiet and peaceful day, without a gunshot fired, ended soon after the trucks had left the city. As the sun began setting, Serbian forces began firing.

Projectiles, rockets, mortars, and tanks—everything seemed to be fired at the same time, all the possible deadly artillery that could be used in a war.

The target?

The building where the UN convoy had unloaded its cargo of food. Unfortunately for us, we were detained in the same building.

We were sitting in our room when the first projectile hit the high school building a hundred yards away. The second one exploded on the roof of the building where my family used to live. Debris bombarded our building.

We didn't wait to see where the next one would land. We ran out to the stairway and into the basement.

We were all in the basement, huddling together and trying to find some protection from the explosions and shrapnel. The building, built in the early 1960s, shook with every detonation. I expected it to soon collapse and bury us alive in its rubble.

We didn't have sandbags to cover the basement windows, only cardboard and wooden boards here and there, so shrapnel simply flew in, hitting the basement walls. Around me I found pieces of metal, still hot from the explosions. One such piece of shrapnel ricocheted off the walls and wounded a man who was hiding deep in the basement.

The explosions filled the basement with clouds of dust that smelled of gunpowder. I thought we would all suffocate

Not My Turn to Die

and die. The only way to breathe was to cover one's mouth with a shirt. Some projectiles exploded not more than five yards from the place where we were hiding. The air pressure from the detonations strained my lungs. I nearly went deaf and had a hard time hearing for days.

That was the biggest, loudest, and longest cannonade since the war had begun in the city. Projectiles exploded on and around our building every couple of seconds for two hours. After a short break, the cannonade resumed again and again, sounding like a constant, rolling thunder.

The relentless bombings went on for a week. Since our room on the third floor was fully exposed and couldn't offer any protection whatsoever, my family took shelter in a dark and dirty basement room used previously for wood and coal storage.

The small and chilly storage room was now our home. We found some cardboard, put it over a pile of coal, and slept on it. To cover ourselves, we used blankets we brought from our room upstairs. When Sanja and I slept on the floor, our parents slept next to us in turns. There wasn't enough room for four of us to sleep at the same time, so one of our parents would sit in a chair while the other slept. The room was so small that if we wanted to get up and stretch, we had to do it one by one. We didn't have the luxury of walking to other rooms and hallways in the basement. Every bit of space was filled with people hiding for their lives.

I could hear rats peeping, running around, and making scratching sounds. Before the war, several street cats lived in the basements of our two residential buildings, hunting down the rats. Now, the cats suddenly disappeared when the bombs began falling on the city, perhaps in fear for their own lives, and the rats became the kings of the underground. At least there was no light to see the rats. We could only hear them. And feel them scurry past us.

It wasn't the artillery shells exploding or the rats that terrified me the most. It was the harrowing cries of the people in the basement who succumbed to hopelessness. They gave me chills. And there was always someone crying—the two women whose husbands were arrested and murdered by the police a few months before, the pregnant lady whose husband was killed by the police too, a mentally ill girl who constantly screamed and cried, blaming everyone around her for all the hardships, or my grandma, who cried because Sanja and I had to spend our childhood in a dirty basement.

Thoughts about life before the war constantly swirled through my mind: playing soccer and basketball with friends, going to school, swimming in the river in the summertime, feeling the warmth of the sun, breathing the fresh air, seeing the sky, being able to eat anything I wanted and do anything I wished.

I used to take all this for granted. It seemed so natural before, but so distant and unreachable now.

During the week we spent in the basement, seventy-six of us used two bathrooms on the second floor, since it was too dangerous to go to the third floor of the building. I always waited until the last moment to use the toilet. For days, we hadn't had enough water for drinking, and we couldn't even think about flushing the toilet. The squalid smell of urine and feces forced my stomach to turn every time I went to the bathroom. But my stomach was usually too empty for me to throw up.

We had only ten gallons of water during this week, and we used it only for drinking. Nothing else. No face and hand washing, no brushing teeth, nothing. The only food we ate that week was some old bread my mom had toasted in the oven in the first days of the war. The relatives of our neighbors who now lived in our apartment had smuggled a plastic bag of that bread to us a few days before the cannonade began on the neighborhood.

For the seven days while the brutal bombing went on, I saw hardly any light. A small window in our storage room was covered with cardboard and wooden planks. I couldn't tell if it was day or night outside. We were in complete darkness. I saw light only when my parents lit an oil lamp to eat. That time was brief. We had only a drop of oil in the lamp.

My eyes got so accustomed to the dark that when I finally left the basement, I had a hard time keeping my eyes open. For a while, I was afraid I would go blind.

As we lived in a room full of coal, our faces were black, like those of mine workers who had come up from an underground shift. When we cleaned our faces with a wet towel, however, they were so white that they looked as if there was no blood in our bodies at all. My face was so worn and tired that I could hardly recognize it. I was afraid to look at myself in the mirror.

Even after the cannonade ended, there were still "normal" daily bombings of the city. I was sick of the basement and I told my parents I didn't want to go back there even if I had to die. We all went back to the exposed room on the third floor, hoping for the best.

About this time, after two months of detention, the local Red Cross officials finally visited our detention site and brought us some of the food that had arrived in the city via the UN convoy. We were told that the Serbian forces had destroyed only a part of it with their bombs. It was very little food: a cup of rice and flour and about a half a cup of oil per person. But in conditions near starvation, it provided long-awaited help.

The Muslim forces from Goražde started a military campaign called the Circle in mid-August 1992. The goal, as our

Not My Turn to Die

police guards commented in the stairway, was to force Serbs away from the hills and suburbs on the west bank of the river Drina to end the siege. The Muslim forces sneaked out of the city and attacked Serbs from behind. After days of fighting, Serbs withdrew from the territory they had controlled. The Serbian civilians who lived in territory controlled by the Serbian forces also moved away.

After Serbs left the suburbs and hills on the west bank of the river Drina, the brutal orgy of vengeance began. First, Muslims from the city looted Serbian houses located in the territory previously controlled by Serbs. Serbian belongings appeared around the city—furniture, cars, food, electronic devices, clothes, and cattle. Then, when there was nothing left to steal, almost every single Serbian house was torched. About a thousand houses burned down in only a week. From the building where we were held I could see the houses burning in the suburbs west of the city. During the day, I saw enormous clouds of smoke, while at night countless flames lit the sky. We soon began hearing stories of many Serbian civilians, most of them old, ill, and not able to move, who stayed in their homes in territory previously controlled by the Serbian forces; it was said that they were all brutally murdered, most of them never properly buried. Some Muslim friends told us about the corpses lying around Serbian houses in villages near the city.

One day a man called Kula, the man who had wanted to slaughter our friend Nedim on the day in June when my parents were taken hostage, appeared in front of our detention building. I watched him through a hole in a window in the building stairway on the second floor. I heard him bragging about burning the Serbian Orthodox Church, which had been built in the fifteenth century. Laughing, he explained to people gathered around how he and his unit broke the heavy church door, smashed icons, and finally set the church on fire. Then he said he needed a car to go somewhere. He smashed a passenger window on a car parked outside, and when the car wouldn't start, he came into our building and requested that the police send someone to push the car in order to start the engine. The police ordered some of us, including my father and me, to go out and help. We did as we were told. After about ten yards of pushing, the engine started and Kula drove away.

Later that day, the same police officers told us that Kula had driven the car to one of the suburbs, where he broke into a Serbian house and attempted to steal a canister of homemade brandy. Behind sat a land mine, set up to explode when someone moved the canister.

It was there that he was gravely wounded. When he couldn't receive adequate help in the Goražde hospital, a group of his fellow soldiers and friends hiked over the mountains, carrying Kula in a handbarrow. It was said that he died when they arrived at a hospital in Sarajevo.

The revenge for more than three months of Serbian attacks and bombings was dreadful. With their scorched-earth tactic, the Muslim officials from Goražde wanted to make sure that, if Serbs ever decided to return to their homes after the war, they wouldn't have anything to come back to. But the war was far from over. The Serbian forces still held their positions in the suburbs and hills on the east bank of the river Drina.

It was early morning in the first week of September and the eight of us were sleeping in our room. Sanja and I slept in one corner on the floor, which our parents thought was the safest spot in the room. I was sleeping right next to the wall.

Suddenly, there was a massive explosion. It felt and sounded different from all the previous ones. There was a thud and a very loud detonation, and I could feel a strong hit that shook the building.

We woke up abruptly. No one knew what had happened or where the projectile had hit. We were all disorientated, not knowing what to do. Finally, someone yelled to run outside and toward the basement. We didn't have to change, since we slept in our clothes, always ready to run, even in the middle of the night.

Other people were awake too, many already in the stairway on the first and second floor. Sick of the basement, we stayed there.

After about an hour, a policeman who came to the building to start his shift told some of us to peek outside and see what had happened. I went outside with my Dad and a few other people. Hiding behind a garage, I saw a scene that shocked me. The projectile that woke us up had hit the building precisely where our room was, leaving a big hole in the wall.

I froze. My whole family had been there.

I turned around to look at the battered surroundings, which bore the brunt of months of fighting and bombings. There was no building that wasn't hit by artillery shells. Half of the roof on my primary school was missing. Across the river, I saw that the minaret, a tall tower on the main Muslim mosque, had been destroyed. I took a look at the building where we were held. The walls were pockmarked with shrapnel and bullet holes. Debris was scattered all over the neighborhood, with pieces of brick, glass, metal, and other wreckage everywhere. The city and the neighborhood where I'd played in my childhood were now hardly recognizable.

Not My Turn to Die

My dad and I went back to our room to see how the wall looked from the inside. I was terrified when I realized that the projectile had exploded right where my head lay while I'd been sleeping, on the opposite side of the wall. The last row of four bricks in the wall hadn't totally blown up, and that was what had stopped the projectile from getting into the room. If it had gone through, it would have not only blown up my head but killed my entire family as well. The last bricks were pushed halfway inside the room, and only the wallpaper kept them together.

We were blessed that the projectile hadn't hit the wall directly, but obliquely. If it had been a direct shot, not even a wall six bricks thick would have saved us.

The Muslim forces from Goražde completed their military campaign, called the Circle, by the end of September 1992. After days of fighting, they conquered the territory near the city center on the east bank of the river Drina, forcing Serbs to a point about seven miles away from the city.

Again, there was massive looting after the Serbian forces and civilians retreated. The main street that led to the mostly Serbian-populated suburb called Bare bordered the detention building, and I could see crowds of people carrying stolen goods. I'd never seen so many people on the streets in my city. They were like ants, moving in a constant stream and carrying everything one could possibly imagine, from TVs, clothes, and food, to house doors, windows, and furniture. I even saw two young men hauling a doghouse.

About fifty houses burned down after Serbs evacuated, but not all. The police chief quickly moved into the area with his police force, and even though they ignored the mass looting, they prevented people from burning houses. It was a wise move. Goražde was overcrowded after the arrival of refugees, many of them still living in schools. Not burning Serbian houses as an act of revenge provided proper housing for a number of Muslim refugees.

Military victories by the Muslim forces in August and September 1992 were significant and relative at the same time. Muslims gained more territory and confiscated many weapons and food supplies left behind by Serbs. They also forced the Serbian forces out of the hills surrounding the city center, the source of daily sniper and artillery fire for the previous five months. At least the snipers weren't able to fire on the city streets anymore and people were able to move around freely. Projectiles still often exploded in the city, now fired by Serbs from longer distances. Even though the territory controlled by Muslims in Goražde was now larger, the city was still under siege, cut off from the main Muslim territory in central Bosnia.

One morning in early October, the police chief came to the detention building and told us that we would be released the next day. We had hoped and prayed every single day to leave this place and the terrible conditions in which we had lived for four months. However, leaving posed a problem for many Serbs, who had nowhere to go. When these people were arrested, they had taken food and clothes for three days and locked their houses and apartments. During the time we were detained, many of their homes had been ransacked. All the food and valuable possessions had been stolen and many

Not My Turn to Die

homes had been usurped. When dispossessed people asked the police to help them to expel those who had seized their homes, the police said there was nothing they could do.

My family was lucky to have in our apartment Muslim refugees whom we knew and who had promised to protect our home. They had taken care of our apartment and possessions like they were their own. After our release, they immediately moved to an empty apartment above ours whose owners had left the city prior to the war.

My grandparents and our friends Mitar and Dragan had bad luck. Their homes had been usurped. My grandparents were never able to enter their home again, even to collect family photos. Great photographic memories of sixty years of traveling and bringing up three sons and six grandchildren were gone forever.

People who had nowhere to go after being released found refuge with other Serbs whose homes were available. My grandparents and Mitar came to live with us, while Nenad moved in with another Serbian family in our neighborhood. There were now seven of us in our apartment. That was a luxury after having had eight people living in one room and sharing a bathroom with no running water with twenty people.

7

In only a handful of instances in the four months we spent in detention did I not feel hungry when I went to bed. On those long and gloomy nights, I would lie on a thin mat on the floor thinking about my favorite foods. For hours, I would turn from side to side, my stomach growling and rumbling and preventing me from sleeping.

After our release, the situation didn't look any better. We had no food left in our home. During the fall of 1992, we depended on the generosity of some good people. Even though no one had enough food, some Muslims, on many occasions, gave us a portion of their food. Sometimes they were people who had been our friends for years. At other times they were people my grandfather had helped in the past. And sometimes we barely knew them. Their generosity kept a spark alive in the darkest moments when we had nothing and there was no hope on the horizon that we would find any food soon. So many times we went to bed hungry, knowing there was no food left for the upcoming day. We'd wake up in the morning and just sit around, no one in the mood to talk. To our amazement, in many such moments, someone would show up at our door with a loaf of bread or some other food.

One morning we had nothing to eat for the day, not even a morsel of food. We all sat in our living room, looks of desolation on everyone's faces. It was to be a long day, burdened with hunger. At about ten o'clock someone knocked on our door. My mother opened it and found a woman standing outside holding on to a bicycle. Mom didn't know her.

"Hello. My name is Fatima. Are Nikola and Jovanka here?"

"Yes, they're inside," my mom said.

My grandfather came out and recognized her.

"Hello, Fatima! Come in. It's great to see you after so long," he said. When my grandfather had been a director of one of the companies in the city, Fatima's husband had been his driver.

"Please, could I leave the bike in the hallway of your apartment? I don't want someone to steal it. I have to go back home later," Fatima said. She lived in the suburb called Kopači, about three miles north from the city center.

"Of course. Get the bike inside," my mother said.

A basket was fixed to the bike, with a big plastic bag in it, secured with ropes. Fatima started untying it.

"I wish I could have visited you before, but I had some relatives staying in our house," Fatima said. "I had extra milk and cheese and decided to bring you some."

She began pulling food out of the bag and placing it on the table—a plastic bag full of potatoes, a large piece of dry meat, a loaf of wheat bread, a plastic container filled with milk, another container with cheese, and cookies.

"You said milk and cheese. There is so much more on the table," my Grandma said.

"I hope you will like it."

"With this food, you are saving our lives. Thank you so much. I hope we will be able to reciprocate one day," my mother said.

"Please don't even think about that. I'm glad I can help you in these hard times."

"This morning we woke up knowing we had no food even for the kids. Now you showed up with all this. This is a miracle!" my grandfather said, pointing at the table.

"I woke up this morning and decided to come. I just felt like I had to do it today," Fatima said.

I stared at the food on the table. I was hungry. I hadn't eaten since lunch the day before. Soon, Fatima saw me staring, opened the box of cookies, and gave it to Sanja and me.

We ate one cookie each. We didn't want to show our guest how desperate and hungry we were. After she left, all of us had a great meal: a slice of bread with some cheese.

The schools opened again after the Muslim military victories in the city, but only for the Muslim kids. The Serbian children, about ten of us that remained in Goražde, didn't go back to school.

When two Serbian women whom we met when we were detained went to the primary school where they had worked for decades, they were told by the principal that they couldn't continue teaching. The school didn't want Serbian teachers anymore.

My parents never went to talk to the school officials. If the schools didn't want Serbian teachers, they wouldn't accept Serbian students either. And the school officials from my primary school, who knew my parents and knew we had stayed

Not My Turn to Die

in the city, didn't bother to check why my sister and I didn't go to school, even though primary school was mandatory.

While the children from my neighborhood were at school, my sister and I stayed at home. From our window, I could see them walking to and from school, backpacks on their backs, discussing homework. Not long before, we had all gone to the same school together.

Muslim officials also discriminated against Serbian employees in every government institution and company in the city. Eventually employees were told over the radio to return to work. The officials said no one would be paid, but the companies would help workers with food. To people pressured by hunger and scarcity, that sounded fair enough.

My mother went to the company where she had worked for fifteen years. While her Muslim coworkers went back to their offices or were assigned to new tasks, my mother and other Serbs were told that they couldn't work there anymore. My dad couldn't continue with his business either. All three of his stores were destroyed.

My parents hadn't had any income since May, and it was now almost the end of the year. We had some dinars, the currency used in Yugoslavia before the war, but they now had no value. Some German marks we had when the war began were almost gone. Even though we had survived months of endless sniper and artillery fire, attempts to kill us, and starvation and near-death experiences in detention, we were now facing an indefinite period of hunger.

In their agony, my parents started rapidly losing weight. Before the war, my father weighed 215 pounds and my mother 170 pounds. By the end of 1992, my parents had lost almost half of their original body weight. Dad had lost more than ninety pounds, and Mom sixty-five pounds. They couldn't wear their own clothes anymore. Instead, they wore my clothes. Dad, a man in his forties, was able to wear my pants and shirts. I had just turned thirteen. They both looked like the survivors of the Nazi concentration camps in World War II that I had seen on TV before the war. They were skeletons, with bony arms, scrawny cheeks, and lifeless eyes receding into their sockets. Their hair, black only a few months before, was now gray. My grandparents, Sanja, and I were also losing weight, but not as much as Mom and Dad. Sanja and I discovered recently that we now had some gray hair too.

Soon, my parents started arguing. They blamed themselves for not leaving Goražde.

"Why did we stay in the city? Why didn't we realize what was going to happen? How could we have been so naive to let our children stay here?" my mother would often ask, sometimes crying.

"We didn't know what was going to happen. Who would expect it would be like this?" my father would answer.

"It's our fault our children are suffering today. I wouldn't worry, if only Savo and Sanja were somewhere safe," my mother would argue.

Their arguments would get worse and they could barely talk to each other whenever there was an intense food shortage or someone terrorized us. Every day was harder.

Since the first day of the war, Goražde had been totally surrounded by the Serbian forces and cut off from the rest of the Muslim-controlled territory. The only way one could get in or out of the city was by hiking over the mountains to get to Sarajevo, the Bosnian capital, controlled largely by the Muslim forces. People called the passage "Allah's trail."

Stories circulated that, to get to Sarajevo, people had to hike for more than twelve hours through hostile Serbian territory over barely passable mountains filled with land mines. They couldn't take the easiest routes, but had to use the hardest, including thick forests, because they were safer. Convoys were frequently attacked by the Serbian forces. We heard that when it was cold and snowing, people still used the trail, and many froze and died in the mountains. Neighbors talked of their treks and of seeing people who died from cold. They claimed that all of them died with smiles on their faces.

Neighbors also said that, on the way to Sarajevo, every person had to carry a few pounds of munitions and bombs produced in Goražde's munitions factory for the Muslim forces there. On the way back to the city, people had to carry on their backs, together with the food and other merchandise they were bringing back for their families, a few pounds of weapons for the Muslim army in Goražde. This was a payment for the passage. The trail was also used for evacuation of wounded people who couldn't receive help in the Goražde hospital.

By the end of 1992, rumors began spreading around the city about Mayor Hadzic. People were whispering that he tried to escape from the city through the mountains. Even he could not bring himself to stay in the completely surrounded city. Hadzic and some of his close associates were arrested by the Muslim military in the mountains on the way to Sarajevo. The Muslim government ordered his release, requesting that the military in Goražde help Hadzic reach Sarajevo. They did, and Hadzic escaped, leaving behind more than sixty thousand people, both citizens of Goražde and the refugees from the neighboring cities, for whom he was supposed to care as their elected mayor.

Mayor Hadzic, who was believed to be responsible for the arrest and killing of many innocent Serbian civilians in Goražde, and who ordered our arrest and merciless detention, was welcomed in Sarajevo as a hero. He immediately became a deputy prime minister in the Muslim government. Soon, we heard on the news that the prime minister was assassinated by a Serbian soldier while driving in a UN armored vehicle. To our complete bewilderment, the government statement read that Hadzic would be the next prime minister.

The UN convoys carrying food and medical aid started arriving frequently in the city by the end of 1992. They supplied tens of thousands of people with food and medical aid. Without their help, many people in Goražde would have certainly died from hunger.

Once a month, like everyone else, my family would receive some grain or flour, rice or beans, milk powder, cooking oil, and a can or two of meat that looked and smelled like dog food. We would get wheat and rice packed in bags with American flags and a big USAID logo on them and labels saying that the expiration date was back in the 1970s. We thought that the Americans probably cleaned up their storage warehouses and sent us this food instead of throwing it into the garbage. It didn't matter to us. It was still food. We ate what we had on the table and were grateful we were still alive.

To get flour for bread we ground up grain using a small manual coffee grinder. It was too expensive to go to a mill, which would keep about three pounds of flour after grinding thirty pounds of grain. We would turn the grinder with our hands in turns. It would take us about six hours to grind enough flour for a large loaf of bread.

We used the food extremely carefully to last until the next month, when the local Red Cross would, we hoped, give us another share. Whenever the fighting intensified, the food convoys would be delayed, sometimes for weeks. When this happened we had only one small meal a day. Some days we would go without any food.

Our usual diet consisted of two thin slices of bread a day and some rice or bean soup. Dinner became a sporadic luxury reserved for the times when we would somehow get extra food. My parents often tried to give Sanja and me more to eat than they would have for themselves, but we always refused.

Since the food shortages were our everyday life, we never threw away anything that could be eaten. I ate the smallest breadcrumbs that would gather on the dining table after cutting a loaf of bread. My mother never had to wipe off the table.

I would be desperate and fatigued after going hungry for days. Having nothing to do but think about hunger just fueled my hopelessness. In many such moments, I would wander around the apartment in the hope of finding a forgotten can of meat or any other food. I would search in vain all the drawers and shelves in the apartment and look under the beds and couches. Not finding anything, I would spend the rest of the day feeling miserable.

One cold, wintry morning, my grandfather went out to check if the Red Cross would soon distribute any food. It had been a month and ten days since they had distributed small portions of oil, flour, milk powder, grain, and rice. Even though we economized greatly, trying to extend the food, after a month all of it was gone. The last few days my mother boiled three red potatoes and cut them in halves, so every person could get half a potato a day. Now, even the potatoes were gone.

Depressed, cold, and hungry, Grandpa, who learned from the Red Cross staff that some food might be distributed in a couple of days, decided to walk home. On the way back, he met Ibro, his Muslim friend. When Grandpa was in one of his management positions, he had helped Ibro get a job.

Back home, Grandpa told us about their meeting.

Not My Turn to Die

"I met Ibro and his wife on the way to their village. They were going to walk for about fifteen miles to start readying the land for the food-growing season. They said they had to start early since they would have to clean and harrow the land by hand.

"They asked me about life and how we coped with food shortages. I told them we've had little or no food for days. Ibro said he would help if he could, but they didn't have enough food for their family either. He said he would try to help us in the summer.

"We talked to each other for a while, and before they left, Ibro said they had only a loaf of bread they had brought to eat while working in the village over the weekend. He asked me to take it. He said it was for Savo and Sanja.

"I refused, but he took the bread from the bag, handed it to me, quickly said good-bye, and left. He didn't give me any time to refuse.

"Here is the bread," Grandpa said, and put it on the table.

The loaf of bread sustained us for almost a week.

The story Grandpa told us helped me realize that people cannot be divided into groups by ethnicity, religion, or any other feature, only into groups of good, bad, and indifferent people. In my mind, I put Ibro and his wife on the top of the group of good people.

This event also helped me learn something very important about my grandpa. He must have left such a positive mark on Ibro's life to have him willingly give up his only food, the food he had planned to eat with his wife over the next few days.

Ever since the war began and the electricity went off, we had cooked using a wood stove. All the firewood and coal

Not My Turn to Die

stocks we had in our basement had disappeared before we returned from detention. We had to find a way to get some wood for cooking, but more importantly, we had to come up with enough firewood for the winter. Winters in Bosnia get very cold, with snow and freezing temperatures from late November until early March.

My father found a Muslim man who owned a truck and who transported for us a truckload of wood in exchange for a pack of twenty cigarettes Dad had hidden somewhere. A few of our friends helped us cut and collect the wood since we couldn't afford to pay for this.

To find firewood, we drove about three miles outside the city. All the forests surrounding Goražde had already been cut down. Sitting in the back of the truck, I could smell the burning cooking oil, as if someone nearby was preparing fried chicken. Since the war began, all the supplies to the city, gas included, had been cut off by Serbs. When the gas became scarce and too expensive, people began driving cars and trucks using cooking oil, which was cheaper and more available on the black market ever since the UN food convoys began regularly arriving in the city.

Like the lawlessness in other aspects of life in Goražde, cutting trees resulted in total mayhem. All the hills surrounding the city, especially the areas where the Serbian population had lived, were now treeless. Only months before, the city was surrounded by beautiful forests. The city's population needed firewood for the upcoming winter, but the officials never did anything to organize the people to prevent destruction of all the forested areas. No one cared about the future. The uncontrollable tree cutting soon caused severe erosion and floods, especially during rainy periods, when water and mud poured from the surrounding hills straight onto the city streets.

Not My Turn to Die

In my home, we stopped commenting about such anarchy. Our fellow citizens had been stealing from neighboring shops and the homes of their Serbian neighbors. Refugees had been burning books stolen from the city library. Thousands of Serbian houses had been burned to the ground. Even the graveyards had been desecrated. The police, who hadn't stopped certain criminal acts, had, nonetheless, killed many and held in detention the rest of the Serbian civilians who stayed in the city, most of them old people and children. So the destruction of nature by our fellow citizens came as no surprise. By then it would have surprised us if someone had wanted to preserve it.

On December 31, 1992, we had very few reasons to celebrate. The only reason to be happy was that we were all still alive and no one had been wounded yet.

Only a year before, I'd been in my grandparents' home, celebrating New Year's Eve with my sister and our cousins. We had always gathered there. Now my grandparents were living in our home. Our cousins were who knew where. The last time we'd heard from them had been nine months before.

The whole day I'd heard fighting and explosions in the distance. It seemed as if neither side wanted to take a break from fighting, if only on this international day of celebration. While people around the world celebrated with their families and friends, people in Bosnia and Herzegovina continued brutally killing one another.

Since we never had enough firewood to heat the whole apartment, we heated only our living room, and spent days

Not My Turn to Die

there. At night, we slept in cold bedrooms, covered with many blankets, which kept us somewhat warm.

On New Year's Eve, we all sat in the living room, lit only with a small oil lamp, and talked about our past celebrations.

Just before midnight, a barrage of bullets sounded in the city. It started somewhere on the west bank of the river Drina. It sounded as if dozens of guns were firing, with explosions from time to time.

"Either someone is celebrating the New Year or there is real fighting," Grandpa commented.

"Let's just hope that they don't come over here," my mother said.

"There is nothing else we can do but hope," my father said.

The firing sounded louder with every second that passed, definitely moving toward our neighborhood. I was now able to clearly hear people singing and chanting.

"Allah Akbar!" This is a Muslim religious phrase meaning "Allah [God] is great."

"For whom? For Allah! Against whom? Against the chetniks! Against Serbs! Allah Akbar!"

Wild screams and intense gunfire followed the chants.

My mother turned off the oil lamp, wanting to leave the impression that no one was in the living room. We sat in total darkness, silent. People outside were now yelling, hysterically laughing, singing, and shooting their guns somewhere around the police station, about sixty yards from us. The fact that the police were there didn't seem to bother them.

"Come out, police! Cowards! Stop hiding in your basement. That's all you've done since the war started. Go fight the chetniks as we do," the voices outside screamed.

Some ran into our yard, screaming obscenities and shooting.

My nerves were tingling. My hands and knees were shaking. I was telling myself not to be afraid, but my body and my mind didn't listen.

"Damn, I wish we had an apartment on the first floor, so we could jump over the balcony and hide somewhere if they enter our building," my father said.

"Let's move to one of the bedrooms. It's safer there if they fire their guns from the yard," I said.

We moved to the bedroom, crawling on our hands and knees. We left the room door open to hear if they start climbing the stairs in the stairway.

"Please God, be with us and save us now, as you did so many times in the past," I could hear my mother praying. I crossed myself three times and prayed the same prayer.

Minutes seemed like hours. My heart was beating so fast, my body still shaking. I was cold. Freezing.

"Hey, people, why are you so afraid? Come out, you cowards, and celebrate with us. It's New Year's Eve," a man screamed outside.

At that moment a gun fired bullets just under our window. My mother took Sanja's and my hands, moving us both toward her. I listened for the noises from the stairway. I expected to hear them running upstairs and kicking on our door with their boots, like they had in the beginning of the war when they took my parents away.

Nothing. No noise came from the stairway. Only the voices in the yard.

"Let's go. No one wants to party with us here. It's dead," a man in the yard yelled. Someone started singing again, this time a little farther away. The song said that mothers should not mourn if their sons die fighting for Bosnia. They played it on the local Muslim radio station all the time.

It sounded as though they were moving away.

Not My Turn to Die

Minutes passed. We were still. They slowly moved toward the area where the city hospital was, still singing, screaming, and firing their guns.

Thousands of bullets were fired in the air that night in the name of celebration. The next day, we listened to the news reports from Goražde on the Muslim-controlled radio from Sarajevo. The reporter claimed that the city had neither weapons nor bullets to fight against Serbs.

"Goražde was brutally attacked yesterday. New Year's Eve, the holiday celebrated all over the world, wasn't respected by the chetniks. They bombarded the city all day. We don't know how long we can defend the city without weapons and munitions. We don't ask the world to fight for us. We only need weapons to fight the enemy."

I was outraged. I couldn't believe my ears. The truth was shocking enough; they didn't need to make up lies to get the world's attention.

"Someone listening to this radio report in another city or another country might think that Goražde is really a city that is defending itself with a couple of guns and a dozen bullets," my father said.

"They can say anything they want. They are the only voice from the city. There is no one to tell the other side of the story," my mother added.

"If the problem was genuine and if they were so desperate for munitions and weapons, they would save the bullets from last night's celebration and use them to defend the city," I said.

My family, being Eastern Orthodox Christian, celebrated Christmas on January 7, according to the old Byzantine calendar, in which almost all religious holidays come two weeks after those celebrated by Roman Catholics and other Christians.

Christmas of 1993 was the first one my family celebrated according to the religious traditions. My grandma helped us in this, remembering Christmas celebrations from her youth. Ever since my parents had survived being taken hostage by the terror squad, we all felt blessed to be alive, and we began thanking God for saving us and praying for our survival and peace. We weren't religious before the war, and we hadn't become religious overnight, but we assumed that besides the enormous luck we had had, there surely had to be something more. So far, God or some divine power had helped us survive countless missile explosions, snipers firing around us, oppression, and starvation.

My mom surprised us greatly on this Christmas Day. The day before, she had gone to a marketplace to get some food. She had been saving a small bag of coffee for a special occasion and decided that Christmas was it. Coffee was scarce; people drank coffee made out of roasted wheat. Real coffee was a delicacy. Mom was able to exchange it for a small bag of potatoes, two pounds of meat, some flour, a few eggs, and a bottle of milk. Mom and Grandma cooked a great meal with potatoes and meat, baked a loaf of bread, and even made a small cake. After ten months, we had a meal similar to the meals my family had eaten when we lived in peace. Before the meal, we all gave thanks and prayed to God to help us survive the war and to give us freedom.

The lunch seemed longer than any other before. We ate the food quietly, savoring it, overwhelmed by the dining table and our plates full of delicious food. It brought back memories of the good food we used to eat.

Between October and February, I did not leave my home. During that time, Sanja would sometimes go out with her Muslim friend Elma.

"Don't play with *her*. She is our enemy," kids would say to Elma in front of my sister. Eight-year-old Elma just ignored them. She never called my sister by her name when they went outside and other people were around. She didn't want to reveal that Sanja was a Serb.

Sanja never told Elma about our food shortages. Elma had heard about them on her own or her parents had told her, and she often invited Sanja to her place and had her stay for lunch. Even though they also didn't have much food, they had much more than we did.

Unlike my sister, I refused to go out. After thugs and the police had terrorized my family so many times over the course of previous months, I didn't feel I was living in the same city. I no longer felt safe anywhere. I didn't know most of the people in my neighborhood anymore. Most of them were refugees. Those people I did know I didn't feel like I knew anymore. I knew many of them hated my family. They lied that my parents were spies, that they should be killed. Some talked about this even in front of us.

I started seeing my city and the majority of the people in it in a different light than before the war. They were now a source of degradation, forcing me to lose all connections to the world outside my circle of family and close friends.

Our closest friends now were some of our Serbian neighbors and people had we met in detention: our neighbor Slobodanka, Mitar, Dragan, Vlado, and a few other people. They were all adults, close to my parents' age. Their children had left the city before the fighting broke out. For months now, they hadn't known about their whereabouts. They often talked about them and how much they missed them. My parents always reminded them that it was better that they weren't here; they wished Sanja and I weren't here with them, that we were somewhere safe.

They would visit us almost every day and listen to the news on the radio or play cards and chess with us. We listened to everybody's news: Serbian news, Muslim news, Radio Free Europe, Voice of America in our language. Then we discussed and compared the newscasts. Every time we heard about negotiations between the warring sides, our morale and our hopes would be high. After a while, we understood that, no matter how bad the situation on the ground was, no matter the suffering of the people or the pressure from the foreign governments, the politicians couldn't even sit at the same table to talk, let alone negotiate a peace agreement and stop the war.

Dragan and I began studying English from my sixth-grade textbook and a dictionary he found somewhere. Every few days we would meet and study the basics or try to improve our conversational skills.

Often, I would watch kids playing in the yard through the windows in our apartment, hiding behind the curtains. They played all the games I had played there not long before. Some of them played basketball at the hoop I made with my friends and put above my dad's garage door. But most of the time I read books. I read almost all the books we had in our home. In a way, reading helped me escape. I read works written by Milan Kundera, Ivo Andric, Ernest Hemingway, and many other writers.

I read Ivo Andric's *The Bridge on the Drina,* the winner of the Nobel Prize for Literature in 1961. The book traced the deep-rooted conflict that had existed in the Balkans ever since the Turks occupied the region in the fourteenth century. After reading the book, I understood that this war was a mere continuation of centuries-long animosity between Christians and Muslims living in the area.

Some books, like Hemingway's *The Old Man and the Sea,* I read a few times. I was amazed by the old man's persistence in his struggle with the big fish on the open sea. Even though my sister and I had a large collection of children's books in our home, I never opened any of them. I did not feel like a child anymore. I couldn't go back to reading children's books. Instead I listened to the news, read adult books, thought about survival, and talked about serious issues with my parents, my grandparents, and our visitors.

Like my sister, I had only one Muslim friend in Goražde during the war. It was my neighbor Mirza. While I was spending months in the apartment, Mirza often came and asked me to go out with him. I always refused. I would have liked to go out with him, but I disliked the surroundings full of hate and discrimination. When he realized that, he would come and visit me, but not insist anymore on me going out.

For days, Mirza and I experimented as electricians. We wanted to come up with a source of electric energy. He told me he'd seen small machines that people designed to produce electricity. He said it worked. Our parents laughed at us, but we kept working.

Mirza brought an old bike to my apartment, and we turned it upside down and fixed it to an old table my dad had on our balcony. We used a car-motor fan as our energy producer. We fixed the motor to the old table and put an elastic string over the bicycle wheel and the motor. Turning the bicycle wheel would at the same time turn the rotating part of the motor very fast and produce an electric current strong enough to recharge batteries or power the radio.

Our machine worked well. Every few days we would spend an hour turning the pedal by hand and recharging our batteries. Our parents didn't have to ask people who worked in the city hospital, which had electric generators, to recharge their batteries anymore.

It was February 1993 when I couldn't take it anymore. I was sick of being in the same place for so long. It felt like being in prison. I had to end my self-imposed isolation and get out, no matter what.

One day I offered to help my mom bring water from the well inside the police station. She was surprised, but I told her I had to go out.

Outside, my legs moved strangely. It felt like I didn't know how to walk properly anymore. I ignored the people outside. I didn't want to see their faces. I looked straight ahead.

We went to the same well I once went to with my dad in the beginning of the war. This time there was an electric pump, since the police had electric generators, so we didn't have to haul the water up manually.

Every once in a while I would go to the well across the street to get water. I also went to Mirza's apartment next door. It wasn't very much, but it was progress after four months of confinement in my home.

People don't have to be killed or physically tortured in order to suffer greatly and be humiliated. Verbal assaults, psychological pressures, stripping people of their human rights, and public dishonoring can sometimes be even more painful than actual torment or death.

In the beginning of 1993, the Muslim government in Goražde began assigning Serbian males who remained in the city to small squads and forcing them to do hard labor. They used them as slaves to do all the dirty work they could come up with.

Digging trenches in the fighting zones and cutting trees to heat municipal government buildings were somehow bearable activities. But forcing my father and other well-known and respected Serbs to sweep the streets of Goražde, the city where they had been born and lived all their lives, was a blatant exploitation intended only to destroy their human dignity.

There is nothing wrong with cleaning city streets. Some people do it for living. But for the Muslim radicals in Goražde, the purpose of cleaning the streets wasn't to have a clean city. No one really cared about the environment. They had destroyed most of it by then anyway. They wanted only to see distinguished Serbs, who only months before were painters, teachers, journalists, and lawyers, cleaning the streets of their city, so the Muslim extremists could laugh at them, point their fingers, and do to them whatever they wanted. If my father and his friends ever responded to the insults and derogatory comments, the extremists could beat them, even kill them, without ever being held accountable. Individuals with small minds had come to power, and there was nothing to be done but quietly hope to survive and wait for better days.

After a day of humiliation on the city streets, my father would come home miserable and exhausted. We knew that he was suffering, both physically and mentally, but he always kept it inside himself. He didn't want to overwhelm us with his stories of degradation. He thought we already had had enough.

Digging trenches was more dangerous and physically demanding labor. My dad often went to work on empty stomach. The officials drove him and other Serbs to the fighting zones in an open truck, where they would spend ten hours digging. Depending on the guards on a particular day, they would sometimes get two slices of bread. Whenever he got the bread, my dad, who was extremely skinny and weak at the time, ate one and brought the other slice home for my sister and me to share.

Most of the time though, the guards were ruthless individuals who spent their days pointing guns at workers and talking to them in an insulting way. Their only goal was provoking an angry reaction. One evening Dad told us that the guards said they could kill the workers at any time without fear of being held responsible. "We just have to say that you tried to escape and we shot you," they said, adding that they wouldn't do that anytime soon since they needed them to dig more trenches.

My dad and the other workers never responded to the guards' comments.

Dad would come back home after digging trenches hungry, cold, and worn out. Often, he had to go back and do the same hard labor the next morning. Still, I never heard him say that he hated or wanted to hurt or kill someone for all the horrific things that had been happening to him and his family.

In late February 1993, my dad got sick. By this time, he had lost ninety pounds and his body seemed too weak to endure the fever. He spent ten days in bed, his face pale and his body shivering with cold. He often couldn't walk to the bathroom on his own. One of us had to walk with him to make sure he didn't collapse. I helped Mom when she would change Dad's clothes, which were wet with sweat. He was so skinny. I could see his entire bone structure and count all of his ribs.

This was a very hard period for all of us. We thought he would die and we weren't able to help him. His body temperature was dangerously high. We didn't have any medications, vitamins, or ingredients to make him even a soup. There was no point in taking him to the hospital. They didn't have enough medications for the seriously ill and wounded. Dad drank unsweetened tea and ate bread and some old boiled potatoes once or twice a day.

By the end of the week, at the point when he almost lost consciousness, my grandfather went to the city hospital to consult Dr. Beslic and see if he could come to see my dad. Dr. Beslic was our family friend. He stayed in Goražde and worked day and night in the city hospital. He was the only doctor performing surgery in the surrounded city for a very long period of time. He told us that many times when he performed surgery there were no anesthetics to reduce people's pain. Even amputations of arms and legs had been done many times without any anesthetics and painkillers. He often had to use a metal whipsaw during such operations.

Dr. Beslic came with Grandpa to see my dad. Upon realizing my dad's condition, he got angry, telling my grandparents and mother that they should have called him earlier.

"Here are some pills for Slavko. I know this is not enough, but that's all I could find. He has to take them regularly for the next few days. Please give him a lot of tea and make him hot soup every day. Also, if you have any food rich in vitamins, that would be helpful," Dr. Beslic said.

"Slavko wouldn't get so sick if we had ingredients to make him soup and proper meals. We only had potatoes and bread," my mother said.

"God, why didn't you call me earlier? I don't understand why you waited so long. It might be too late now! I will see if I can help," Dr. Beslic said. Then he left.

That same evening, Dr. Beslic sent one of his friends with two big bags of food full of vegetables and ingredients for soup.

After a week, Dad got better. The food and medications from Dr. Beslic saved his life. He could now walk on his own. It took him a month to fully recover. When he was able to go outside, he paid a visit to Dr. Beslic. When he thanked him and promised to repay him one day, Dr. Beslic told him to forget about it. He told him that friends should be there to look after each other, no matter what.

A few days later, my dad had to go back to digging trenches and cleaning city streets.

People had been greeting one another for decades with the phrases "Good day" and "Good afternoon" when Muslim radicals in Goražde decided to try to prohibit these greetings as something that "dirty Serbs" and chetniks used. Instead, people were to use Muslim religious greetings or say only "How are you" in greeting one another. Many Muslims resisted the bizarre campaign, saying that "Good day" was a worldwide greeting and had nothing to do with Serbs. Still, a large number of people in the city bought into the absurd lie. People either blindly believed the propaganda or didn't want to be called "chetnik-loving" traitors.

One day, my mother and our neighbor Slobodanka went to get water from the well inside the police station. When they reached the well, a policeman approached them. He greeted them with "*Merhaba.*" *Merhaba* is a Muslim religious greeting.

My mother and Slobodanka replied with "Good afternoon."

"What did you say? That dirty Serbian greeting is prohibited in this city. If you don't want problems, you better change," the policeman yelled at them.

Slobodanka told him to use whatever greeting he wanted and that she would use what she had been using all her life. He screamed at her to do what she was told or she would suffer the consequences.

No one from my family had been physically abused for refusing to comply with the new rule, but many Serbs, especially old and powerless people, had been beaten on the city streets for saying "Good afternoon." An old man, a distant cousin of my grandma, visited us after he was beaten while standing in a line for water. He was guilty of saying "Good afternoon" to a friend. A Muslim man standing nearby hit him in the face and two other men joined in, giving him a few slaps and saying that they would kill him the next time he said "Good afternoon." They knew he was a Serb. The man who hit him first lived in his neighborhood. When the old man came to our home a few days after the incident, his face was still swollen. He had a black eye and scratches on his forehead.

One morning our Muslim family friend Adil surprised us with a visit. Adil lived in a village where we had our cabin, about fifteen miles west of the city.

"I'm glad to see that you are all alive and unhurt," Adil said as he entered our home. He and my grandpa Nikola had been friends since their youth.

Adil was one of my favorite people. Prior to the war, my family would spend almost every weekend at our cabin. Adil worked as a manager of the only grocery store in the area, and my sister and I got presents from him every time we entered the store. He loved children and always had great stories to tell about his and my grandpa's childhood.

I remembered him as a tall and strong man, but now he looked completely different. Adil was in his sixties, but his haggard face and sunken cheeks made him look as if he was in his eighties. As he walked in, I could see that he could barely move his right leg. He carried a wooden stick in his hand.

"What brings you to the city?" my Grandpa asked.

"Nikola, my dear friend, a great need forced me to walk in pain for miles."

"We heard from someone that you and your wife have health problems, and that you can hardly walk," my grandpa said.

"My legs hurt, but I'm good compared to my wife. She has been ill for months now, not able to get up from bed. I came to get some medications for her," Adil said.

"Couldn't you ask someone to go to the hospital instead of you?" my Grandma asked.

"Not many people live in the village anymore," Adil said. "It's only us, old and weak, who stayed. Younger people left."

"Do you have any food? Who's working the land now that both of you are ill?" my mother asked.

Adil didn't answer. Instead, he started crying.

"Remember . . . remember the wealth and luxury in which we all lived." Adil wept. "Whenever my friends came to visit me, I would roast a sheep. Now that's all gone. My wife and I are ill, and no one can work the land. We've only one cow that keeps us alive with its milk."

I wanted to cry. My family was in a very bad situation, oppressed and often hungry for days, but he was totally broken and defeated.

Still crying, Adil told us, "I don't know if you heard this before, but I have to tell you that your cabin was burned down a couple of months ago."

We all looked at one another. Some time before, we had

heard that some refugees were living in our cabin. No one had told us about it being destroyed.

"Nothing is left of it. It's as if it never existed," Adil added.

The cabin was built mainly of wood, with white bricks outside. In my mind I could see it clearly. Some of my greatest childhood memories were formed at the cabin. Every so often, my relatives and friends would visit us there and we would play all kinds of games. It seemed that the beautiful green hills were reserved only for us and our fun. Now it was gone as if it had never been there before. That's what the war was doing to all of us. Destroying lives, memories, friendships. . . .

My father broke the silence: "That's the reality we all live in today. I can only hope we all survive unhurt, so we can build another cabin."

I couldn't sense any sadness in the tone of Dad's voice. It was hard to grieve over a cabin when misery and tragedy were so common.

"I don't know who burned it down. Some say it was Muslims; others say Serbs did it," Adil said.

"It's not important anymore. What's happening to all of us is one big disgrace!" my father said.

Later that day, my grandfather went to the hospital with Adil, where he got medications for his wife. After that, Adil met with some people who promised to drive him to a spot near his village. He still had to walk, old and ill, a few miles farther to get home.

———

We woke up one morning knowing that there was no food in the house. This was becoming normal. Everyone but my sister was in the living room, deep in thought. Sanja was in the bedroom.

Not My Turn to Die

All of a sudden, Sanja appeared, a huge smile on her face. She held her left arm behind her back.

"We won't be hungry today," Sanja said and showed us what she was hiding in her hand. It was a small plastic bag, in it, about three pounds of grain.

"Where did you get that?" Mom asked.

"Every time we would get our ration from the Red Cross, I would take a handful of grain and hide it. I was hiding it for a moment like this," Sanja said.

"I thought we wouldn't eat today," I said. "Let's grind it and bake bread."

Mom baked a loaf of bread that lasted for a few days.

The next week there was the same hunger and feeling of desperation. We had no food, no money, no one to ask for help. Everyone we knew was also struggling.

It was a cold, windy day outside. My dad had left to do hard labor. Grandpa and Mitar were somewhere outside.

We had had a piece of bread and a cup of unsweetened tea for lunch the day before. Nothing after that. It was now approaching lunchtime. I longed for anything. Bread, boiled potato, a biscuit, fruit. Anything that would satisfy my hunger.

First Grandpa came home, then my father. We wondered where Mitar was. It was almost dark outside. He usually came home before dark.

It was around seven when Mitar appeared at the door. I opened it, holding an oil lamp, and realized right away that he didn't have his blue winter jacket on. He was shaking.

"What happened to you? Where is your jacket?"

"Let me get in and warm up first. Then I'll explain."

He was holding something. It was a big bag, one of those USAID bags for grain, rice, and flour.

Mitar sat by the stove in the kitchen, the bag in front of him. He was still shivering from cold.

Not My Turn to Die

"What happened to your jacket?" my dad asked.

"You won't believe what happened to me. I was walking across the bridge, on my way here, when a young man approached me and said he liked my jacket. I told him it was my only jacket, my most valuable property remaining. He said he would give me twenty-five pounds of grain for it. I thought for a moment and said yes. At least he didn't strip it off my back. This grain may help us prolong our agony," Mitar said.

"You can look into my wardrobe and pick any jacket, anything you want," my dad said.

Everyone was hungry. We quickly ground up some grain. We couldn't wait for the dough to rise to bake bread. Dad made pancakes for dinner; two pancakes per person. There was no syrup, jam, or anything else to spread on the pancakes, only two tablespoons of sugar for all of us. It didn't matter. They were still delicious. It felt great not to go to bed hungry again.

In the spring of 1993, the American and NATO military forces started dropping food supplies over the Goražde area from their airplanes. Most of the food landed on the hills outside the city via parachutes, at night, and in huge pallets. They began this campaign because they were unable to secure regular safe passage for the food convoys through the Serbian-controlled territory.

Hungry, residents of the city went out searching for the food pallets. In the beginning, the search wasn't organized and people wandered around the hills looking for food that fell from the sky. After about a month, the city officials decided to organize groups to search for food and collect it. My father and other Serbs forced to do hard labor were the first to be called in.

Still not fully recovered from the fever that had almost killed him, and terribly thin, Dad would leave home every morning at six o'clock and come back at six in the evening. Trucks would take him and other workers outside the city, where they had to walk for about ten miles a day searching for food pallets.

Soon, armed gangs and private militias organized themselves and began collecting the food and selling it on the city's black market. They would spend nights patrolling the area in their trucks and listening for the airplanes flying above. After finding some of the food, they would secure the area and shoot at anyone who tried to come close.

People from the city spent nights in the hills that weren't controlled by gangs, waiting for the food to fall. My father often said that it looked like the whole city was out in the hills. People were desperate and would do anything to get any food on the table, even if they had to risk being killed by gangs and militias.

My dad had never stolen anything in his life. But forced by hunger and starvation, he began taking small amounts of the food dropped from the airplanes and hiding it in his shirt, pockets, and pants. He even made secret pockets in his pants and jackets where he would hide the food. One day he would bring home a few cans of tuna or meat, and another day some rice or flour. I never considered this stealing. The food was dropped for all the citizens of Goražde, but often only a few would get it. My dad took only the small share that he believed belonged to us.

One day after collecting the food in the hills, my father came home with a horrified look on his face. Not even changing from his work clothes, he sank to the couch in the living room, speechless.

"What happened? Did someone attack you today?" I asked.

He didn't answer.

"What's wrong, Dad? Why do you have that expression on your face, like you've seen a ghost?" I asked again.

"I wish it was a ghost and not those poor people," he said.

"What people? What happened? Please tell us," my mother said.

"This morning, we came to an area where the planes had dropped the food the previous night. A family, the parents and two kids, were sitting around a fire, waiting for a food drop. It landed on top of them." He stopped for a moment. "They were killed instantly. Blood and limbs were everywhere. There was blood mixed with the flour from the broken bags."

"Did you know them?" my mother asked.

"Someone said their names, but I forgot. People who came with them were sitting nearby. They saw everything."

My mother sat next to him on the couch and held his hand. We left them alone.

One night, when our neighbor's boyfriend came home drunk, he burned two of my father's cars, which were parked outside. My dad had used them for his retail business before the war.

Since Selma, our neighbor, lived above us and there was only see-through plastic on the windows, we could clearly hear them whenever they raised their voices.

"You stupid bastard, didn't I tell you not to do any harm to Slavko and Gordana's family or other Serbs in the building? Why did you set the cars on fire? Take a gun and fight in the war instead of terrorizing innocent people," Selma screamed.

"Don't defend those dirty Serbs. They forced you to leave your home and become a refugee."

"These people don't have anything to do with that. Why would I blame them for what happened in my city? They weren't there."

"They should all be killed. They are all the same to me," he said.

My dad couldn't do anything about the burned cars. We didn't need more trouble.

Selma's boyfriend wasn't the only one causing us trouble. Some of Selma's friends, who spent a lot of time partying in her apartment right above us, were the most notorious terrorists stationed in Goražde during the war. They were a paramilitary group called HOS. About fifteen of them had come to Goražde over "Allah's trail" by the end of 1992.

It had been a well-known fact in the city that this group had been responsible for many massacres of civilians committed in Serbian-controlled territory. Everybody talked about it. The story went around that on Christmas Day of 1993 they sneaked behind the Serbian forces and entered a village where they slaughtered all the women, children, and old people. Most of the males from the village were members of the Serbian forces and weren't in the village at the time of the massacre. We also heard news reports that claimed the same.

The HOS soldiers never kept their actions secret. They were proud of what they were doing, repeatedly bragging publicly about it. I often listened to their conversations in the yard or Selma's home, especially in the evenings when the weather was pleasant in the spring and summer. I'd sit on a small chair in our kitchen, with a window slightly open.

"Man, the little blond girl you slaughtered in that village wasn't more than five years old."

"Did you hear her mother screaming while she watched me killing her child?"

"Oh, yes. We should do that more often, where we enter a village behind the front lines and have enough time to do whatever we want."

Another day, while sitting in the kitchen, I heard their conversation in Selma's apartment upstairs.

"I heard that Serbs live in the next-door apartment and in the apartment downstairs. Let's go and kill them all," a man said.

They shouted out a battle cry, cocked their guns, and fired in the air from Selma's windows.

I froze. I couldn't move or say anything. I wanted to tell everyone in the apartment what I had just heard, but nothing would come out of my mouth.

I heard them opening the door upstairs and yelling that they would kill all Serbs they came across. Some of them stayed on the floor above, trying to break into another Serbian apartment. Others ran downstairs to deal with us.

While they screamed and kicked at our door with their boots, I heard a familiar voice. It was Selma, screaming hysterically.

"How many times have I told you that you can come to my place but you can't harm my neighbors? What in the hell are you doing now? This is my home and I make the rules. If you don't like them, leave."

"We just wanted to have some fun."

"I don't care what you do when you leave this building, but while you are here, you can't touch my neighbors," Selma screamed.

I have no idea how Selma was able to control those whose job it was to terrorize and slaughter people. I only know that they listened to her. After that, they would come, drink, scream, and fire their machine guns from Selma's apartment, but they never again tried to break into our apartment and kill us.

Not My Turn to Die

It wasn't only my family who feared the HOS terror squad. Our Muslim neighbors lived in dread from them too. People were afraid to let their kids play in the yard while the thugs drank in Selma's apartment.

A Muslim friend of my grandfather came to visit us one day. Not long after he arrived, Selma's friends started screaming and firing from the apartment above us. I could see Grandpa's friend moving nervously on the couch.

"I don't know if I can stay longer. I have some business to do. Do you think it would be safe to leave now?" he said and got up to go.

"Maybe you should wait until they calm down," my dad said.

Suddenly, one of our neighbors yelled from the yard, saying to the HOS soldiers that they should stop firing their guns before innocent people got shot.

A moment later, I heard them running, the sound of their military boots echoing in the stairway. Passing our door, they yelled that they would find and kill the person who had raised voice at them. As they ran outside, my mother and sister were just coming back from a well with canisters filled with water. The HOS monsters stopped them in the yard, assuming in their drunken minds that the two of them had complained about the gunfire.

"No one ever tells us what to do. Drop the canisters and walk in front of us," one of them screamed.

My mother wanted to say something, but an HOS soldier yelled at her, "Shut up and walk toward the river."

Scared to death, I watched all this from our window.

Out of the blue, one of our Muslim neighbors, a refugee from a nearby city, came out of the building.

"Please don't hurt them. They weren't in the yard when you fired. It was a man who yelled at you. He walked away toward the police station. Leave the two of them alone. They did nothing," our neighbor pleaded with the drunken soldiers.

"I think he's telling the truth. I could swear that I heard a male voice yelling at us," one of the thugs said.

Without saying anything else, they ran toward the police station, looking for the person who had yelled at them. My mother and sister, not even knowing what had happened and who had yelled at whom, grabbed the canisters and ran into the building.

Grandpa's friend, who was in our apartment while this was happening in the yard, couldn't believe what he had just witnessed. As soon as my mom and Sanja entered the apartment, Grandpa's frightened friend took his jacket, said good-bye, and left.

Some time after the incident, he met my grandfather again. "Nikola, you and your family are the bravest people I've ever met in my life," he said. "I was with you only for an hour, and those were the most horrifying moments of my entire life. You've had to go through hell for more than a year."

Spring and summer became our favorite periods of the year, because that was the time we could find plants that we cooked or ate fresh. Everyday food shortages forced us to become wild food gatherers on the eve of the twenty-first century. The two plants we ate the most were weeds—stinging nettle and dandelion. Whenever there was a quiet day, we would walk a few miles outside the city in search of edible plants. If we were in luck, we would bring home bags full of stinging nettle and dandelion. Late in the summer, we even found fruit and wild mushrooms.

Not My Turn to Die

On the way to the deserted Serbian villages where we searched for plants, we could see the destruction from the summer of 1992 when Muslim forces took over the area and destroyed everything. Roads were littered with first stolen and later abandoned goods from Serb-owned houses. Small family graveyards, often located near the main roads in Bosnia, were utterly ruined. I didn't see a tombstone shaped like a cross that hadn't been crushed. The grass around houses and on farms was tall and dried out from the sun. No one was there to take care of it. Broken furniture, rusted metal, clothes, books, and family photos lay littered in the yards. Every single house we passed by had been burned down. Roofless walls and piles of bricks, concrete, wood, and debris were everywhere.

Ironically, the ruins were the best places for finding the stinging nettle.

Having only a little bit of flour most of the time, my mom would often bake bread using ten tablespoons of flour, some salt, cooking oil if we had it, baking soda, and lots of stinging nettle. The flour was there only to help with the consistency. Another meal Mom often made was dandelion stew. She would boil dandelion greens in water and add oil, salt, and a couple of tablespoons of flour. The stew tasted almost like spinach. This was often our sole meal, enabling us to survive the periods of extreme food shortages.

Since we rarely received any yeast for bread from the Red Cross, my mom used sodium bicarbonate from fire extinguishers to bake bread. My dad's friend who had been a firefighter in his youth told us that many people in the city simply opened the fire extinguishers, taking the sodium and using it to make bread and brush their teeth. I heard people discussing whether the sodium in the containers was good to use and if it had any other chemicals added to it. My dad always said he didn't want

Not My Turn to Die

to know if something was mixed with it. We didn't have anything else to use for baking bread and brushing our teeth, and we felt better thinking that the sodium we had to use wasn't poisonous.

For months now, we had had no soap or shampoo. Now and then, the Red Cross would give us some laundry soap. We used half of it to wash our clothes and the other half to wash our hair. Most of the time we washed our hair with a strange liquid my grandma said they used in her youth, right after World War II. She would take a handful of firewood ash from the stove and soak it in water. After a day, she would filter the ash out. We would wash our hair with the remaining liquid. Our new "shampoo" would make our hair stiff. I also found out that our shampoo was actually very acidic, and using too much on your head wasn't recommended. I used it excessively once and burned the skin on my forehead. It was red and itchy for days.

By the summer of 1993 salt was very difficult to get. That was the period when salt became very expensive, and we had no money to buy it. We could live without oranges or chocolate for years, but living without salt would ruin our health. For at least ten days, we ate bread and other food completely without salt. One day, a friend visited us and told us about her neighbors who had the same problem and had found a way to produce salt on their own.

People would take a mixture of the small stones and salt used to scatter over icy roads in the wintertime, put it in water, and wait for the stones and dirt to sink to the bottom of a pan. After a day, they filtered the water and left it to boil for hours. After boiling, the salt would emerge on the surface and could be gathered easily with a spoon. The salt was then placed on a plate in the sunlight to allow the water to evaporate.

My father got a bag full of stones and road salt from a friend who found it in some old storage and we began our experiment.

Not My Turn to Die

For days, our apartment looked like a small lab. Pans with the stone and salt mixture immersed in water were scattered everywhere in our kitchen, boiling on the wood stove, or drying on the balcony. The process took a long time, but it kept us healthy. In a week, we were able to produce about two pounds of salt, which we used carefully to last as long as possible.

There were, of course, other shortages.

Goražde had a highly controlled economy during the war —a marketplace where goods were exchanged. People would bring meat, vegetables, oil, salt, sugar, and flour, and customers would purchase them in exchange for cigarettes, gas, coffee, clothes, or German marks.

Local currency didn't exist since the war began. For some reason, most people didn't like American dollars, British pounds, and other currencies; they trusted only German marks.

Gold, silver, and diamonds were not worth much then. My mother discovered this when she tried to exchange some of her gold jewelry for food. No one wanted it. People laughed and said that the gold and other jewelry was the last thing they needed at the moment.

Prices were much higher than normal. Goražde was under siege and it was hard to get food and supplies to the city. Cigarettes were the most expensive goods. A pack of twenty cigarettes would sell for up to one hundred German marks (about fifty U.S. dollars at the time). Flour was about four marks per pound and salt about ten marks per pound. Prices often fluctuated, depending on the frequency of the UN convoys getting the food to Goražde as well as the extent of fighting around the city. Most of the food sold in the marketplace were goods delivered by the UN. Someone was making huge profits on people's misery.

Having neither food nor money forced us to consider selling or exchanging our possessions. We had to eat, and the only way to get food was to sell our belongings that had any value. There was always the danger that anyone could come and take them from us anyway without any consequences, so it was better for us to sell our possessions if we could.

We first sold our car, a Russian Lada, for four hundred German marks, even though it was worth far more at the time. This one wasn't burned by our neighbor's boyfriend since it was hidden in our garage. The money paid for enough food for almost two months. Other possessions we exchanged directly for food. My parents would tell our Muslim friends that we had appliances to exchange for food and they would spread the word among the people they knew. We exchanged our color TV for the equivalent of one hundred German marks and got a bottle of cooking oil, eight pounds of flour, three pounds of rice, and five pounds of beans. The rest of our valuable possessions left our home in this way.

One day, a newly married Muslim couple came to our home. They said that our neighbors had told them we were selling things.

"I love the crystal wineglasses and the painting on the wall. Can we get those for a bottle of oil and ten pounds of flour?" the lady asked.

My mother thought for a moment. "Yes, you can have them."

The lady turned toward her husband. "There will never be a better time to get things for the house."

He nodded.

When the couple left, I went to the room and looked at the empty wall where, moments before, the oil painting had hung. My parents had received it from friends when they had moved in about fifteen years before. At least the newlyweds didn't just take it for free.

By the end of 1993, our home was almost empty, with only couches, beds, large cabinets, and a few kitchen supplies left. My mother even insisted on selling presents she and my dad had received from family and friends on their wedding day. We all resisted, but she persuaded us to exchange them. She got a few pounds of rice, beans, and flour for the treasured presents.

Mom also exchanged all of Sanja's and my shoes for food. We couldn't wear them. They were too small. Some of our friends whose children had left the city before the war brought us a few pairs of shoes. I kept one pair. It wasn't my style, but at least I now had something that I could fit on my feet.

We never felt bad about exchanging everything we had for food. Some of our Muslim neighbors said we were crazy for giving away our possessions for close to nothing. They couldn't see that the food we received in return kept us alive. Our Muslim neighbors got extra food for either working or being soldiers. We had none of those options. They could go over "Allah's trail" to the mountains surrounding Sarajevo and bring food in backpacks. We couldn't.

One day, when my mother went to the market to exchange clothes that had become too small for my sister and me, some people asked her if she knew anyone who had new or even used male underwear to exchange for food. My mom came home and told us.

"Why don't you make underwear?" my father asked.

"What do you mean?"

"We can find a sewing machine and you can make underwear from bedding. No one will mind if the underwear isn't original with a trademark. People need it!"

"Well, why not. A man told me today that half of his village would buy it," my mother said.

Not My Turn to Die

A friend of ours had an old German sewing machine his great-grandma had used more than fifty years before, but it was still in good condition. To operate it, one pushed a pedal with one's foot. Dad and I brought it to our home and my mother started sewing. She used my shorts as a model. She would make a dozen sets of underwear, take them to the market, and exchange them for food. She usually got cheese, eggs, flour, milk, and vegetables, significantly enriching our diet.

Soon my mother taught my father how to sew so they could make even more underwear. This lasted for a while, until we had only one set of bed linens per person in our home.

8

***

very single day we thought about escaping from our war-torn city. My parents often said that they would already have tried to escape if my sister and I hadn't been with them. Goražde being under siege made an escape almost an impossible task. In the first months of the war, snipers shot at anyone moving around. To successfully escape, one had to be invisible to the Serbian snipers and to the Muslim police and army. One person might succeed, but we were a family of four in a small city where many knew my parents' identities.

When the Muslim army pushed Serbs away from the suburbs and hills surrounding Goražde in September 1992, the task of escaping became even harder. If we wanted to flee now, we would have to walk a formidable distance—at least ten miles in any direction—to get to the fighting zones, and then cross the battle lines without being seen. And then, of course, there were the land mines planted everywhere by both sides.

Nevertheless, some people escaped. Back in November 1992, a young man who was detained with us in the summer of 1992 somehow escaped. His advantage was that he was alone.

In May 1993, our friend Mitar, who lived with us, left our apartment one morning, and never came back. At first, we feared that someone might have killed him. After he'd been missing for two days, my parents checked his belongings and found that all the documents and photos he kept in a box under his bed were gone. We hoped and prayed that he had escaped and was already a free man.

Three days after Mitar disappeared and failed to show up for forced labor, the police came to our home, summoning my father and grandfather to the police station. This also happened to other Serbs who were Mitar's friends. The police placed them in different rooms and interrogated them for six hours. They used classic police scare tactics, telling every one of them that the others had already confessed to having helped Mitar escape. The police wanted to know how he had escaped and if any Muslims had helped him. My father and grandfather and the others were unable to tell the police anything because they truly didn't know anything.

I woke up one day with an extremely painful toothache. I went to see a dentist who said she would have to pull the bad tooth out. The dentist's name was Danica, and she was Serbian. She and her husband came from Serbia to Goražde before the war, where both had found jobs. She worked in the hospital because there was still an acute shortage of medical workers in the city. Her husband, though, did forced labor with my dad.

Not My Turn to Die

She seemed more optimistic than most people. She talked about her little daughter, who had left the city prior to the war, and was living with her parents in Serbia. Danica was now six months pregnant and hoped the war would end before her second baby was born.

She pulled out my tooth without giving me any anesthetics. There simply weren't any, even for surgeries. It was the most painful experience I ever had. Afterward, she said another tooth needed urgent care and promised it would be less agonizing. She told me to come back in a week at nine o'clock in the morning, when the electric generators would be working at the hospital.

I woke up early on the day I had the scheduled appointment and got ready to go. I wanted to leave before nine and to arrive before she got busy. When I was about to leave, my parents told me to have some breakfast.

"You won't be able to eat for a while after she fixes your tooth. And who knows how long you'll have to wait. Better eat something now," my mother said.

It was five minutes before nine. We all sat at our dining table, eating breakfast. Suddenly, I heard projectiles being fired in the distance. Only this time, the firing sounded different, fast, like machine-gun fire. I counted more than ten.

"What's this? In a year of war, I've never heard such a roar," my father said.

We looked at one another, waiting for the explosions. We had stopped getting scared about the bombings a long time before. We would hear them whistling through the air, but we wouldn't even try to hide. In many instances people got wounded and killed while hiding in basements. If our destiny was to die, we believed, there was little we could do to prevent it.

The projectiles started whistling frighteningly through the air. It sounded like a wild, unbearable scream, one we had

151

not yet heard in Goražde. Soon, one after another, they slammed into the city. Never before had our furniture trembled like that from explosions, even when the projectiles had exploded in our yard. This time, everything was shaking as if there was an earthquake.

"I guess I'm not going to see the dentist today," I said.

"Of course not. They might fire again. Stay where you are," my father said.

The projectiles that massacred many people on that morning had been fired by Serbs from the Russian-made rocket launchers called Katyusha. These launchers are considered one of the deadliest small conventional weapons, with the ability to fire thirty-six large rockets almost instantaneously.

Later that day, a friend of ours visited us and told us that one of the projectiles had hit the city hospital, killing and wounding many people. Among the victims was my dentist, Danica. If I'd finished breakfast earlier, I would have left before nine and been in or just outside Danica's office when the projectile exploded. If they had fired only ten minutes later, I would have been there with her when they hit. She had come to work before nine, and shrapnel had killed her while she was cleaning her equipment and getting ready for me and other patients to come in. Her baby couldn't be saved.

It was late April of 1993 when we heard on the radio that the United Nations Security Council in New York voted to make Srebrenica, a small town in eastern Bosnia, a safe haven with UN protection. Srebrenica, reports claimed, had been under siege ever since the war had started, with a large number of Muslims surrounded by the Serbian forces.

Not My Turn to Die

In the following weeks, we patiently listened to the news, hoping to hear that the same decision would be made for our city too. Goražde had also been under siege for almost a year now.

Finally, in the beginning of May, Goražde and four other cities under Muslim control were also made UN safe havens. With this proclamation, we expected the fighting would stop and we would be able to freely leave the city.

Days and weeks passed and nothing changed. The city was still attacked and bombed by Serbs. I still saw fully armed Muslim soldiers roaming the city as before, even though the news reports said that the first condition for establishing safe havens was a complete demilitarization of the surrounded cities. We hoped the UN forces would soon arrive in the city, set up a base, prevent the two sides from fighting, and establish safety. This was, after all, one of the safe havens.

But the UN forces never came. They, and the International Red Cross, only established small offices in Goražde, a few people in each.

We hoped they could arrange some kind of exchange. We figured there were probably Muslims trapped in a similar situation in a territory controlled by Serbs. They could let them go free and we could leave Goražde in return.

My parents and some of our Serbian friends immediately visited both offices, asking the representatives there to help us leave the city. They asked the UN and Red Cross officials about a possibility of an exchange or if they could drive us about ten miles outside the city and help us to become free people again, with our human rights and dignity restored.

Neither the UN nor the Red Cross personnel ever agreed to help.

"We aren't here to interfere in politics. Your case is extremely complicated and political. If we help you leave the city, we'll be accused of supporting ethnic cleansing," the

International Red Cross officials told my parents during one of the meetings.

"But we want to leave. We'll sign any papers saying that we are leaving willingly. I don't care how someone perceives our departure. I don't want to sacrifice my children in order to maintain artificial multiethnicity in Goražde," my father said.

"When we say that we don't want to stay here anymore, what has that to do with politics? People move from one place to another every day. We want to leave this city because our lives are in danger," my mother said.

"If we help you leave the city, you will become refugees, losing your homes and property. Why don't you stay to save what you have here?" a Red Cross official asked.

"I would lose all I have for my children to be safe. You shouldn't worry about our homes and property. We are ready to lose everything we have, just to be free and safe again," my mother said.

My parents couldn't believe how oblivious, uncaring, and unfamiliar with the situation and sufferings of ordinary people the UN and International Red Cross officials were.

"Do you understand at all what we are telling you? We have been terrorized here since 1992. Everyone in this city is suffering, but we are also seen by Muslims as the enemy. Muslim extremists, hit squads, and even the police and government officials have threatened to kill us. The only reason we are oppressed is because we are Serbs. Many innocent people have already been killed just because they were Serbs and remained in their homes. If you don't help us, we'll probably die!" my father said.

This meeting, like many meetings afterward, didn't bring us any help. The UN and the International Red Cross were our greatest hopes for survival when we found out they were coming to the city. But our hopes were in vain. They never respond-

Not My Turn to Die

ed to our pleas for help. They had their procedures and orders from New York and Geneva. Helping ordinary people survive oppression during the war wasn't in their job description.

For more than a year, my extended family didn't know if we were alive or dead. We didn't know about their whereabouts either.

One day my dad got a message from an information center telling him to come in the next day. This center was established to help people connect with their families and relatives who lived in other parts of Bosnia or elsewhere. They used two-way radio transmitters, the only communication devices connecting Goražde to the rest of the world.

My mom and dad went. One of the radio stations was operated by my uncle's former colleague, with whom my uncle had established a two-way radio club years before. He told my parents that my uncle had asked him to contact us.

They were instructed to talk only about family matters. Nothing about war or politics.

Mom and Dad talked to my dad's two brothers. They said both of them and their families were refugees in Serbia, and that everyone was alive and well. My parents said the same about us. The conversation was very brief, lasting only about two minutes.

About a month after my parents spoke with my uncles, we received a small box of food from them through a UN translator who visited Goražde. Hidden in a bag of biscuits, my sister and I found two packs of cigarettes. One pack secured us firewood for the upcoming winter, while the second pack brought a lot of food to our table.

Soon after the arrival of the package, we received a letter from one of my dad's brothers. The people from the local Red Cross told my dad that the letters sent to Serbs in Goražde via the International Red Cross were first checked by the Muslim police censors before reaching the recipients. Sure enough, the letter we received had been opened. Someone had crossed out many words and sentences with black marker. We could hardly make any sense of the letter. Nevertheless, it assured us that our relatives were free and safe and worried about us.

We'll never know how many packages were stolen and how many letters destroyed, never reaching us.

After the letter, all communication with our family stopped. We suspected that someone was deliberately preventing us from communicating by two-way radio and from getting packages and letters.

In the summer of 1993, during quiet, sweltering days, my sister and I sometimes went to swim in the river Drina with a few of our Serbian friends. We couldn't bear to hide in our home anymore. Instead of going to the beaches in the city center where many people could recognize us, we went half a mile up the river to an island in the middle of the Drina, where mainly younger people and refugees swam. There, to our relief and surprise, no one ever bothered us.

The abandoned island used to be covered with tall willow trees and look like a jungle from the Tarzan movies. It was now a naked piece of land. Even the smallest trees had been chopped down to be used as firewood.

My mom and dad came with us once, when Dad had a day off from hard labor. When they took off their clothes, the entire beach turned toward us and stared at them. People whispered in disbelief, asking if anyone knew who the two skeletons were.

They swam once, dressed, and went back home. They didn't want to draw unnecessary attention to themselves or us.

Sitting on the sunny beach and swimming in the light blue water of the river Drina, I would sometimes forget, for a moment, the reality in which I had been living for more than a year. I would close my eyes and imagine normal times when everyone in my country lived in peace and without hate and fear. These daydreams wouldn't last long. Too often, the sound of Serbian projectiles, exploding in the city or even hitting the houses just across the river, would jolt me back to reality. Like most of the people at the beach, I paid no heed to the projectiles anymore. The early fears of dying had changed to feelings of apathy and exhaustion.

One evening in the late summer, I heard airplanes flying above the city. It sounded like yet another delivery of food in the hills by the NATO and American planes. Suddenly, I heard strange noises outside. It seemed as if something was hitting the asphalt in the yard and the roofs on the buildings.

"What's going on?" Grandma asked.

"Are they dropping food on the city? They've never done that," my mother said.

"They are crazy! They'll destroy the city. The food palettes are heavy and could damage buildings and kill people," I said. I was thinking of the family in the hills that was crushed under a palette.

I could hear some of our neighbors calling one another and shouting, "They're dropping food on the city! Come out."

My father, sister, and I ran outside. It was about ten o'clock at night. Dozens of people were already in the yard. The three of us wandered around, not knowing where to go. A half-moon gave us some light to search by. I paid more attention to the sky than the ground, hoping nothing would hit my head.

I saw something that looked like a shoe box near the garages in the yard. When I pushed it with the toe of my shoe, it felt as if something was inside. I took the box in my hands. It was a lunch box, the same type my father had smuggled once after a day of collecting the NATO food drops with his forced labor group.

"Dad, I found a lunch box," I whispered.

"Great. They must be dropping only small, ready-to-eat boxes, not big palettes."

We continued searching the yard, together with many of our neighbors. Sanja found a box too, next to the ruins of the business complex that had burned down a year before.

Planes flew over again, this time dropping their cargo somewhere else. After looking around for a while, we decided to go back home.

"Look what we found," Sanja said proudly when we got back to our apartment. "Two lunch boxes!"

We opened one box to see what was inside. There was a meal of meat and potatoes, some crackers, peanut butter, jelly, snacks, instant coffee, and sugar.

"We can eat some of this tomorrow!" Sanja said.

While the lunch boxes were meant to feed two people, they fed six of us the next day.

———————

One day, a man called Emir came to our apartment. I recognized him right away. He'd been a professional karate fighter. I used to go to the sports arena to watch his fights before the war. When the war began, he became a member of a special unit of the Muslim forces. He had been wounded twice. Recently, we had heard that he had been promoted in the Muslim army. He was highly respected in the city for his military contributions.

When I first saw him at our door, I feared that he had come to oppress us like many others before. As soon as he spoke to my parents, I realized I was wrong.

"Slavko and Gordana, I need your help. My daughter has leukemia and her doctors told me that she will die if she stays in the city. I talked to some UN officials and there might be a possibility to evacuate her from the city. They think that Serbs will ask for something in return. I know you want to leave the city. Would you let your kids go to the Serbian side in order for my daughter to be evacuated?" Emir said.

My parents looked at each other for a moment. "Yes, we would let our kids go. I hope we can arrange it, both for the sake of your daughter and our children," my dad said.

For about two weeks, Emir negotiated with the UN officials, the Muslim government in the city, and over a two-way radio with the Serbian side. He visited us many times during that period. One day he announced that Serbs had agreed. Emir's daughter was to be evacuated to the Serbian capital of Belgrade, where she would undergo medical treatment. With her, my sister and I would be evacuated to Belgrade too, where some of our relatives lived.

Everyone in my family was excited. Over and over again, they said that at least Sanja and I would finally be free.

A few days later Emir appeared and told us that the plan had been canceled. It turned out that the local Muslim government in Goražde didn't like the idea of evacuating his daughter to Serbia.

"Now, after weeks spent organizing this, I have to find another way to evacuate my daughter. If nothing else, I'll take her over 'Allah's trail' myself," Emir said.

For the next couple of days, I felt as if my world had completely crashed. I had put all my hopes into this plan of escape. The thought of my sister and me leaving the city without our parents and grandparents ripped my heart apart, but, as my parents insisted, our freedom would mean freedom for them too, even though they would remain in the city. Now politicians who didn't like the idea of an ill Muslim girl getting medical help in Serbia had dashed our hopes.

Emir went over "Allah's trail" with his daughter, climbing the perilous mountains. We heard later that not long after getting to a hospital in central Bosnia, his little girl had died.

Our friend Dragan, an artist, sold two of his paintings to a United Nations worker in the fall of 1993. The UN officer's name was Fillip, and he was French. Dragan didn't get any money for the transaction. The Frenchman paid with twenty packs of cigarettes. For Fillip, this was a great deal. Instead of paying two thousand German marks, he "bought" the paintings with cigarettes he had purchased for only forty marks before entering Bosnia and Goražde. Many international aid workers profited greatly at this time while the people of Bosnia suffered. Selling only two to three boxes of cigarettes a month, they could at least double their wages.

However, Dragan didn't mind exchanging his paintings for cigarettes. He thought he'd made a great deal too. With twenty packs of cigarettes, one could live a comfortable life for a long period of time during the war. Dragan helped out many of his friends by giving them a pack of cigarettes to exchange for food. He gave us one pack, and with it we were able to get food for at least ten days.

A week after Dragan made the deal with Fillip, he persuaded him to visit my family in our home. My parents wanted to talk to him about our situation in Goražde. For more than a year, the Muslim media had portrayed Serbs who remained in Goražde as loyal citizens who didn't want to leave the city. This was a bald lie. If any way existed for us to leave, we would go right away.

Along with Fillip came his Muslim translator. When we told Fillip that our only wish was to leave the city, he was very surprised.

"The Muslim officials have told me that you are happy here and that you would never leave," Fillip said. "They say you are loyal citizens who support their cause."

"We've stayed in the city because we refused to believe that people who lived together in peace for decades would start brutally killing one another. If we had wanted to be involved in the war, we would be somewhere fighting right now," Dragan said.

"They lie when they say we are loyal citizens. If they thought we were loyal, why did we spend months in detention?" my father added.

"We just want to go far away from this city," my mother said.

"I'm leaving next week. Please make a list of Serbs who want to leave and get it to me in the next couple of days. I'll make sure to deliver the list to the Serbian officials, the media, and the international aid workers in Sarajevo," Fillip said.

Unfortunately, we were never able to deliver the list to Fillip. Two days after he visited us, the Muslim military searched Fillip's apartment looking for the letter, even though they had no right to do this to a UN official. We suspected his translator had told the Muslim officials about Fillip's plan to help us send the list to the Serbian side. Nobody else had been there when we talked about the list. Fillip abruptly left the city on the day his apartment was searched and never returned to Goražde.

Shortly after Fillip disappeared, another UN official arrived in the city. He was an American and his name was Joe. One day, Joe approached Dragan and said that Fillip had told him in Sarajevo about meeting us and not being able to get our list. This time Dragan asked Joe to come alone, without his Muslim translator.

One evening, Dragan and Joe appeared at our door. Dragan said they didn't encounter anyone on the way to our home. We had to meet Joe secretly so as not get him and us into trouble. He was a very tall man, at least six foot four.

Even though we didn't have a lot of food for ourselves, my parents wanted to make our guest feel welcome. My father made pancakes, his lifelong specialty. Luckily, we had some extra flour these days. Only Dragan and I knew some English. I studied English in fifth and sixth grade in primary school. Using our hands and facial expressions along with our bad English, we communicated to Joe the situation in which we'd lived since the war had begun. We explained that our only dream since the war had begun was to leave the city. If we stayed, we told him, we would probably all die.

"We talked briefly with our relatives over a two-way radio some time ago, but we were not allowed to even mention the fact that we want to leave the city," my dad said.

"They keep us here only for propaganda purposes," Dragan said.

Not My Turn to Die

"We adults are used as slaves to dig trenches, sweep streets, and provide hard manual labor," my father added, and Dragan and I somehow translated. "We fear they will use us as human shields if the Serbian forces attack the city again."

Joe said he would help us. He asked if we had the list we had planned to give to Fillip.

"Yes," my father said, opening a book where he had hidden the sheet of paper. "Here is the list."

Joe took the list, looked over the names, unbuttoned his shirt in front of us, and put the list inside the shirt. "This is the safest place to hide it. I promise, I'll do everything I can to help you. I'm sorry I can't help you leave the city, but this list will be on the other side as soon as it's humanly possible."

We never saw Joe again, but we knew he had delivered our list to the Serbian side as he had promised. Just couple of days later, as we listened to Radio Belgrade, we heard a report about Serbs who had stayed in Goražde: "Our credible source informed us that more than one hundred Serbian civilians who stayed in Goražde yearn to leave the city, but the Muslim officials are keeping them there both as a source of hard labor and for propaganda purposes," a journalist said.

Even with strict orders from their UN bosses not to get involved, Fillip and Joe did so, risking their well-paid UN jobs.

We hoped someone on the Serbian side would try to help us now that they knew about us. But days and weeks passed and nothing happened. Not even another mention on the radio.

We were constantly in fear of getting killed as revenge for something the Serbian forces did. Many Muslims in Goražde

Not My Turn to Die

would get furious whenever Serbs attacked the city and killed people. They would react as if it was our fault. There was no point in explaining that we too were in danger of being killed by artillery shells. No one would listen. Propaganda encouraged illogical reasoning, persuading our neighbors and fellow citizens that all Serbs were the villains and enemies.

One night, soon after we met with Joe, we were in bed when someone fired at our home with a machine gun. My mom and dad were sleeping in the living room, which faced the yard, when a barrage of bullets began hitting the walls. Three bullets ended up in our apartment, hitting the ceiling. Another bullet hit the apartment above ours, nearly killing our Muslim neighbor, who was sitting next to the window chatting with two friends. A few bullets missed the windows and ended up in the building wall outside.

The next morning, my dad went to the police station and reported the shooting incident. Two policemen came to our home, looked at the bullet holes, and estimated the location from where the attacker fired. They said that the shots were fired from the yard.

Soon after, some of our Muslim neighbors and friends told us that they had personally heard a man named Meho bragging around the city about firing at our apartment. They said that he claimed that he was the only one trying to eliminate the enemy within and especially my family.

My dad and my grandparents knew him very well. He had gone to primary school with one of my uncles. A bad student, he might never have finished primary school without my uncle's help. After high school, Meho continued to be a friend of my uncles and my dad. Yet, to our amazement, it appeared that he was now waging a personal crusade to exterminate my family. The fact that my father and his two brothers had been Meho's friends for decades no longer meant anything to him. We were Serbs. That seemed to be enough for capital punishment.

My dad went to the police station again and informed the police about the claims that were circulating. They promised to investigate the claims.

A week after this incident, someone again fired at our apartment in the middle of the night. The moonlight was brighter and helped the attacker to see the target better. Five bullets pierced the walls in our apartment. This time the attacker used bullets that explode when hitting a target.

When the bullets began loudly exploding all over the living room and kitchen, I woke up terrified and confused. At first, I thought someone was firing at our front door. Jumping out of my bed, I ran into a wooden desk, smashing into it with my face. Immediately, I felt blood pouring from my nose and mouth.

My parents clambered from the living room to the room where Sanja and I slept. They didn't know the source of the shots either. My grandparents whispered from another room, asking what was happening. Dad whispered back, telling them to get down to the floor and be quiet.

Mom and Dad came close to me and discovered that my face was covered in blood. They panicked, thinking that I had been hit by a bullet.

"It wasn't a bullet. I hurt myself when I jumped from the bed," I told them, blood trickling out of my mouth.

"Keep quiet; they might be at the door," my father said in a low voice. "Put a shirt on your face to stop the bleeding."

We spent the next few hours on the floor in the room, covered with blankets we stripped off the beds. We waited in fear for someone to attack again. Fortunately, nothing more happened. The rest of the night was dead quiet. When we finally

Not My Turn to Die

went back to bed, I couldn't sleep. I spent the rest of the night and many nights afterward listening to the noises coming from outside, expecting someone to show up at our door and kill us. Every bark of a dog, wind moving metal scraps on destroyed and burned buildings in the neighborhood, someone talking or coughing outside, sent chills down my spine. I could hear every sound. We didn't have windows, only plastic bags replacing the glass.

I prayed to God for hours, night after night, to save my family from the horrific nightmare we were in.

The police returned the next day and looked at the bullet holes all over our living room and kitchen. They concluded that this time someone had fired while leaning on the corner of the neighboring building. This gave the attacker a better angle than he'd had the first time. We repeated again the rumors we had heard that Meho was the man who was terrorizing us. They said rumors weren't enough. They needed evidence, they said. Neither Meho nor anyone else was ever questioned or arrested for these two attacks on my family.

Not My Turn to Die

9

The second wartime New Year's Eve and Christmas came and went, bringing nothing good. It had been twenty somber months that we had been living trapped in our city, surrounded by destitution and anguish. For almost two years, my sister and I hadn't attended school and my parents had been without jobs and wages. Food was scarce, and often we went without. For the second time in our lives, Sanja and I didn't have cakes for our birthdays. We craved freedom every day, hoping the tide of darkness rolling over us would wash away soon. After a while, though, the hope slowly began vanishing.

At the beginning of the war, we would be afraid when artillery shells and projectiles exploded in our neighborhood. Not anymore. We just moved from the windows and listened to the detonations, as close as our yard. Hearing about someone being torn apart by projectiles used to disturb us. After a while, such carnage became an everyday reality. Once someone telling us that we were dirty Serbian bastards who should be tortured and killed would have offended and bothered us. Now we didn't care as long as they didn't fire their guns at us and beat us. We weren't braver than before. In fact, I don't think we were brave at all. We only became indifferent and tired of war and suffering.

The second winter was colder than the first. Like they had the first fall, our friends helped us to cut and collect firewood. We helped them too. We paid for the wood transportation with a pack of cigarettes our relatives had sent us hidden in a bag of biscuits. This time we had to go far away from the city to find firewood. The forests close to the city had all been chopped down a long time ago.

There were numerous peace talks, Western ultimatums, and UN resolutions, but not one produced any results. The politicians from all warring factions publicly called for peace, but continued fighting diminished chances for it as soon as any negotiations ended. If they couldn't prevent the war from escalating, how would they stop it now that tens of thousands of innocent people had died on all sides? Listening to the news, I got the impression that the whole world knew about the war in Bosnia. So many international emissaries and powerful countries were involved in negotiations. Yet, there was no peace in sight. Why couldn't the world stop a bloody war in such a small country? How would they ever stop a larger conflict or a world war?

The Serbian forces launched their largest military campaign on Goražde at the end of March 1994. Radio stations reported massive movements of soldiers and military equip-

Not My Turn to Die

ment toward the area. The Serbian officers claimed that they were ready for a final battle to take over the city and drive out tens of thousands of Muslims from one of the enclaves and UN safe havens surrounded by Serbian-controlled territory in Bosnia.

Conquering Goražde, they said, would free thousands of soldiers who held the city under siege, who could be sent to fight elsewhere.

After about ten days of intense fighting, Serbs started pushing Muslims in toward the city. Our Muslim neighbors became nervous, fearing a full-scale defeat. I overheard some of them panicking and discussing the situation in the yard, terrified by the fact that the Serbian forces could soon break through the Muslim defense lines and conquer the city.

Everyone in my home was nervous and afraid too. We feared being used as human shields if Serbs came closer to the city. Another possible scenario was that we would be killed by Muslims if they decided to leave the city center and retreat to the hills on the west bank of the river Drina, something that everyone was predicting.

The Serbian forces tightened their grip and made swift daily progress in breaking Muslim defense lines. The artillery continuously pounded the city. They soon advanced from the east and came very close to the part of Goražde where we lived. The front line was not far away from us. It was possible now to hear the bursts of gunfire and ground fighting.

We listened to both the Serbian and Muslim radio news, trying to better understand what was going on. Not one radio report gave us any reason for hope. They only talked about attacking, defending, fighting, killing, victims, human misery . . .

One news report from early April shocked us more than other news.

"Our soldiers have put explosives in the chemical factory in Vitkovići, a suburb three miles south of Goražde. If Serbs continue attacking the city, they will detonate the factory, causing a catastrophic disaster," a Muslim journalist from Goražde reported.

Many people in the city took this report very seriously. The factory in Vitkovići was one of the largest chemical factories in the former Yugoslavia. It had large tanks for storing chemicals, and many claimed that the tanks still contained significant amounts of nitrogen, ammonia, and ethanol. Nitrogen and ammonia are used to produce explosives, and if those tanks exploded, the whole area would suffer greatly.

Muslims called on Serbs to cease their attacks on the city, but Serbs never stopped. To everyone's great relief, the factory never exploded.

On the news, they also talked about the possibility of NATO forces getting involved in the conflict around Goražde. Some reports claimed that their airplanes stood ready and waited for a decision from the UN Security Council.

A few days of intense fighting passed, with Serbs stepping up their attacks daily. There were no NATO airplanes.

Finally, one day when I heard our Muslim neighbors talking in the yard about huge defeats suffered by their army the night before, two very fast jets appeared out of nowhere and flew very low over the city. The Serbian forces immediately stopped firing missiles.

"They will finally bomb them," I heard someone yelling outside.

"Let's watch and enjoy!"

My family and I, like all the neighbors who lived in the building, ran to the balcony to see what was happening. Two jets flew directly above us in the direction of the area southeast of the city, where the fighting had been the fiercest in the last week.

Soon I heard two loud explosions. NATO airplanes bombed an area not more than a mile away.

"Go on, kill them! Kill all Serbs!" many of our neighbors screamed from their balconies.

"Why did NATO wait for so long? They should have bombed them in the beginning of the war," someone said.

"This will stop their attacks," another neighbor optimistically added.

"It will just piss them off," my dad whispered to us. "When the planes leave, they will continue shelling the city."

It started raining as soon as the NATO planes completed their mission and left. The mood in the neighborhood was not as celebratory as when the planes first appeared. "Is this it?" I heard someone asking outside. "Is this all the help from NATO? They think a few bombs will stop the chetniks? This is pathetic!"

As my dad had predicted, the Serbian forces, incensed by the NATO attack, went on to brutally and indiscriminately bomb the city. It seemed that they fired all the artillery they had positioned around the city. Countless artillery shells and projectiles exploded on and around our building, on the police station across the street, and on other buildings in our neighborhood and the rest of the city. The rain, the fog, the noise created by the projectiles whistling through the air, and the roar of explosions made me think of being in a horror movie. It didn't seem that it would ever end. I wondered if anything would remain intact in the city.

The avenging bombardment lasted for about three hours, sounding like a constant thunder on a stormy day. That night I heard the neighbors saying that the city hospital was stretched to the limit. Only the wounded were brought in. Dead were buried right away in the city parks. One of the burial locations was a park in the yard of a high school, next to the building where my family lived. I saw new graves from our window almost every day.

Whatever NATO's goal was, they didn't stop Serbs from advancing toward the city. Serbs continued attacking during the night and the next morning. Besides endless bombings, I could now clearly hear the armies fighting on the ground. The gunfire never stopped.

A few days later NATO airplanes flew over the area again, in what looked like preparation for another air strike. I looked out our window. An airplane flew over the Serbian-controlled area west of the city when, out of the blue, rockets were fired on the plane. The plane flew upward, chased by two antiaircraft rockets leaving smoky marks in the sky. One rocket found its target. The plane exploded and fell somewhere over the hills on the west bank of the river Drina. I learned from the news that the plane was British and that the pilot had survived by parachuting down. The report also said that this was the first time ever that a NATO airplane went down in action.

"What are we going to do when Muslims start moving to the other side of the river and toward the hills?" I asked my family that night.

Some of our Muslim neighbors told us that they had already packed their bags. Some had even moved their essential belongings to their relatives' homes on the other side of the river.

"We can't just stay and wait for someone to kill us or to take us hostage. We have to try to escape or hide somewhere until Serbs take over this area," I said.

Not My Turn to Die

"I also think we should hide somewhere. But where?" my father asked.

"What about the sports arena?" I asked. The arena had burned down in the beginning of the war, and I knew about the underground passages, which could serve as a hiding place. I had spent my childhood there, playing all kinds of sports.

"What if we go there tonight and have to stay for ten days? What if Serbs never take over the area? What if someone finds us there?" my mother asked.

"I know it's risky, but I don't want to sit here and wait to be killed," I said.

"I agree with Savo. You have to hide somewhere," my grandfather said. "I say 'you,' because Jovanka and I are old and would only create problems. Don't think about us. We'll stay and take our chances here."

My parents were reluctant to do anything, fearing that any hideout could easily become a trap.

New Muslim refugees began arriving in the city center night after night, since it was literally impossible to move around safely during the day. Most of the new refugees went straight to the other side of the river. Everyone thought that the neighborhood where we lived would soon be captured by the Serbian forces.

On April 18, the Serbian forces took control of the hills surrounding the city on the east bank of the river Drina, the same hills they had controlled in 1992. As they had done during the first five months of the war, the Serbian snipers and guns resumed shooting at the city. They also intensified their artillery cannonade.

We heard on the news: "Chetniks are bombing Goražde like never before. Twenty projectiles explode in the city every minute. This might be our last report. We will continue fight-

Not My Turn to Die

ing until we all die," a journalist from Goražde reported on Radio Sarajevo.

Many times I'd felt disgusted by lies broadcast by the Muslim media about the situation in Goražde. So many times they'd lied about the attacks on the city when the situation was calm, sending blurred and distorted news reports.

This time, however, they didn't exaggerate. Sanja and I counted detonations. There were at least twenty a minute. Those were the fiercest days of artillery and mortar fire since the beginning of the war. *Boom . . . boom . . . boom . . .* a never-ending roar.

On April 20, some of our Muslim friends visited us. "Two days ago, two old Serbian women were murdered a block away from here. Yesterday, seven Serbs were killed in Tito Street. Hide somewhere if you can," our friends told us.

"We will be careful, but that might not be enough. There is no way we can confront anyone who comes with a gun," my grandpa said.

I woke up early on April 21, after a night of relentless shelling and fighting. I hardly slept. The fighting zone was so close now that I could even hear Serbian soldiers screaming and calling Muslims derogatory names in between the explosions.

The morning was foggy and rainy, like the whole month of April had been. We sat in our living room opposite the hills from where the Serbian snipers and artillery fired on the city. It was about eleven in the morning when I heard someone yelling in the stairway.

"I hope it's not someone coming for us," my grandfather Nikola said.

Unfortunately, it was.

"Open the door! I know you are in there," a man began yelling, hitting our door with his fist.

My mom looked at us, fear in her eyes. "I'll open it before they break in or fire through the door," she said.

She got up and went to the door. The rest of us sat on the couches in the living room. There was no point in hiding. There was no place in our bare apartment where we could not be found.

As my mother unlocked the door, a man violently pushed it open against her. She stayed behind it.

He was alone. As soon as I saw his face, I knew who he was. The man called Meho. He was a friend of my dad and his two brothers before the war. He had bragged around the city that he would once and forever exterminate my family. He had claimed to everyone that he shot on our home twice a few months before. Wearing a military uniform, he marched inside and pointed the barrel of his machine gun at us.

He stood a few feet away from me. His eyes were blood-shot. He looked like a madman.

My eyes were fixed on his AK-47. His finger was on the trigger. I waited for him to start shooting at us. *I hope we all die quickly,* I thought, my entire body sweating and shaking.

He took a step toward my grandpa, who was sitting in the corner. "Nikola, get up and come with me. . . . Get up! I don't have time," Meho yelled, his voice wild with rage. I could smell alcohol as he screamed at Grandpa.

My grandfather stood up from the couch: "Where are you taking me, Meho?"

"Don't ask me anything or I'll kill you right here in front of your family. You will talk to the chetniks and tell them to stop the attacks. You will make a public statement on Radio Sarajevo. You will tell the world that your life is not at risk from us Muslims. If you cooperate, you and your family might live. If you refuse, I'll take you, your family, and other Serbs to the bridge and kill you," he yelled.

"Are you crazy? You think I can stop the attacks? Who gave you that idea? You think someone will listen to me?"

"You were a powerful man for many years. They will listen to you. Move now. Go in front of me," Meho yelled and pushed Grandpa with his gun toward the door.

Meho was at the door when he turned back to us. "I'll come back for you later. I'll kill you all!"

My grandfather left the apartment. Meho followed, pointing his gun at Grandpa's back.

He never asked my father a question, didn't even look at him, even though he was sitting in the same room. They had known each other for decades. Yet, that morning, Meho acted as if he hadn't even seen my father.

With tears in my eyes, I watched from the window. Grandpa was now in the yard, walking first. Meho was behind him, pushing him with the gun barrel. For the whole time, he yelled at my grandfather: "You'll do what I tell you or I'll kill you."

"I don't care anymore if you kill me. I won't lie to serve your purpose. You and your police and extremists have terrorized us for two years, and now you want me to say that we had a great time here during the war? I tried to prevent the war before it began. No one listened. Politicians only wanted to fight. Now you want me to stop the war? Are you crazy to think that they would listen to an old man?" my grandfather yelled back.

"I gave you a chance but you refused. Now I'll kill you. I'll kill all Serbs. Let's go to Vlado's house and get them. Then I'll get your family. I will line up all of you on the bridge and kill you," Meho said.

He pushed my grandfather to go to the house of our friend Vlado, only a block away. About fifty Serbs had taken refuge in Vlado's house in the past seven days. They had all lived in the neighborhood and had been forced out of their homes after the arrival of the most recent Muslim refugees. Some of them had been seriously beaten by those who had usurped their homes. Vlado had opened his house to them, giving them shelter.

My parents, my grandma, Sanja, and I were in our apartment. We didn't know what to do. Where do we go and whom do we ask for help in a place where most people see us as an enemy?

I could still hear Meho yelling in the distance, but I could hardly understand what he was saying.

A few minutes passed. Everything seemed quiet now. I couldn't hear any voices. Then a machine gun fired nearby.

"He killed Nikola," my grandma mumbled and began crying. All of us cried.

He'll kill all of them at Vlado's house, I thought, *and then he'll come back here and kill us. He'll kill us here or take us to the bridge just as he said.* Still, we stayed in our home. We didn't attempt to hide. Where would we go? We just waited in silence.

Ten minutes later, Sanja yelled from the kitchen window, "Grandpa is in the yard with that man who took him away."

At first, I thought she was joking. I ran to the kitchen to see for myself. Indeed, Grandpa was walking alongside Meho. They entered our building.

"Let's all move to the bedroom. We shouldn't be in the living room when Meho comes up," Dad said.

A few moments later Grandpa entered our home. Alone. He said Meho was in the basement. Grandpa asked if we had any roasted wheat to make them coffee. Grandma found some and went downstairs with Grandpa.

Later, Grandpa told us what had happened:

"In front of Vlado's house Meho ordered me to call everyone out," Grandpa began telling us after Meho had left. "Even before I called them, they saw and heard what was happening and people started coming out of their own will. Soon, about fifty Serbs lined up to be killed. People were tired of the war and torture. They just hoped to end the misery somehow.

"Once everyone was outside Vlado's house, Meho told us to walk toward the bridge. We refused. Vlado yelled at him and told him to kill us right there.

"When others also refused to walk in front of him, Meho started firing around us. Bullets flew around, ricocheting off the asphalt. Luckily, no one was hurt. He never pointed his gun directly at us. He wasn't brave enough to fire at such a large group of people.

"Something happened to him at that moment. He stared at us after firing his gun. He was nervous, his forehead sweating. He looked as if he had just woken up, as if he just now came to his senses. As if he just realized what he was doing.

"Suddenly, Meho decided to let everyone go. He said, 'Go back to the house. I don't want to see any of you.'

"He turned toward me and told me to wait. 'Nikola, I want to drink coffee with you and Jovanka.' Then we came here. I told him to wait for me in the basement. I didn't want him in our home, where he might suddenly change his mind again and kill us.

"While we drank coffee, Meho started crying, remembering how our family had bought milk from his mother for years before the war and how you, Slavko, and your brothers had helped him in school with homework. He was now a completely different person than the one that entered our home this morning and dragged me out.

"Before he left, he said, 'Nikola, I didn't kill you this morning; I couldn't do it. I couldn't do it myself. But I know you will all be killed tonight or tomorrow. Someone will come and kill all of you before the chetniks enter the city.' " My grandfather was quiet a moment, letting that sink in. Then he said, "He is a driver for one of the Muslim military commanders in the city. He is well informed."

That evening, we all sat together in our living room, still shocked by Meho's visit. We brainstormed options for survival available to us.

"After what happened today, I think you shouldn't stay here tonight," my grandfather told us. "Jovanka and I will remain here, but you have to hide somewhere with Savo and Sanja."

"We don't have anywhere to go. The people who could help us are heading to the other side of the river and don't know what to do themselves," my mother said.

"If we stay, they'll come again and kill us," I said.

At about six o'clock, our friends Vlado and Slobodanka came to our home.

"I have told this only to my mother, and nobody else except you will know," Vlado said. "I'll attempt to escape tonight. I won't wait for the monsters to come back and kill me in my own house. Meho and another man fired at my home and tried to set my house on fire last night. My uncle and I were awake and heard someone running around the house. When we checked the first floor, a door was burning. We were lucky to be awake and see the fire. If not, fifty people would have burned inside the house."

"I'm going with Vlado," Slobodanka said.

For about ten seconds, it was dead quiet.

"Vlado, can we go with you?" I finally broke the tense silence.

"I want to go," my sister said. By this time, Sanja was thirteen and I was fifteen.

"How do you plan to escape?" my father asked.

"Well, you all heard the radio reports claiming that Serbs came from the north all the way to the soccer stadium area on the west bank of the river. If that's true, they are almost in the city center. We could swim tonight a few miles down the river Drina, and that should be enough to bring us to safety and freedom," Vlado said.

"Have you seen the river lately? It has been raining for almost a month. The river is flooded like never before!" my mother said.

"And the water must be freezing cold at this time of the year," my dad said.

I caught the look of fear on Mom's face. Among all of us, my mother feared the river the most. She could swim, but she was afraid to go into the huge river at night. I didn't want to swim in the river either, but it seemed to be the only option.

"I saw the river from the balcony just before I came here. I don't know anyone who swam the river when it was that swollen. If it continues raining, it might flood half of the city. Still, Drina is our only chance," Vlado said. If anyone knew the river in Goražde, it was Vlado. He had been a fisherman all his life, the first person to own a speedboat in the city, and the first one to water-ski on the river Drina.

My father responded, "I don't know if we could swim for

a few miles. It's been a month since we've had one meal a day. Our bodies aren't strong enough. Sorry, Vlado, but your plan sounds crazy," my father said.

"I think I have enough life jackets for all six of us. If we go in our clothes, we will still have to swim hard, so don't bring anything else with you," Vlado said.

"You all have to go. Please don't stay here tonight. Jovanka and I are old and we will stay. Don't worry about us. Try to save your family," my grandfather said to my parents.

I looked around the room at the worried faces. "If we are lucky, we could be free tonight. Let's get ready! Our misery might come to an end at last. We might be free and safe again."

We didn't know when the killers might come, so we started getting ready immediately. We didn't have time to think it over or come up with an alternative plan.

Vlado and Slobodanka left to get ready. The plan was to meet in our apartment at nine o'clock and wait for an opportunity to leave the building and run toward the river, hoping to get there unseen.

I felt an extreme rush of adrenaline in the next couple of hours. After two years of terror, humiliation, and starvation, we were finally going to try to escape from the city. We'd finally decided to take our destiny into our own hands.

I went to my room and found a photo of my sister and me when I was four and she was two. I was on a bicycle and she stood next to me in the yard. I wanted to bring it with me, to at least have something to remind me of my early childhood. I took the photo out of the frame, remembering that Vlado said that we couldn't bring much with us. My mother placed the photo with about twenty other family photos in two plastic bags and put them in her pocket. We didn't care about anything else. We just wanted to be free again.

Not My Turn to Die

Vlado and Slobodanka came back some time after eight in the evening. They said they were nervous, unable to wait until exactly nine o'clock—the previously agreed time. Vlado brought a large plastic bag with life jackets.

"We have a problem. I have only five life jackets and there are six of us. What should we do now? I have a small inflatable raft that we can use to hold on to. I'm not sure these life jackets will hold us adults above the water as it is, especially that we are going in our clothes." Vlado said.

"So someone will have to swim without a life jacket," my father said.

We stood in silence. Swimming for miles in a cold river was risky enough, especially considering how weak our bodies were after years of eating so little. Doing it without a life jacket was just too risky.

Mom broke the silence. "Were there any tires left after we sold the car?"

"There are some tires and tubes in the garage. They are old, though. Let's hope at least one tube has no holes," my father said.

Dad and Vlado went to search the garage. They closed the garage door behind them so no one could see they were inside. Using an oil lamp, they searched for a good tube. After ten minutes they reappeared with two tubes and an air pump.

"The tubes look good, but neither one has a valve stem. . . . Let me think . . . There might be one in the bathroom cabinet. Believe it or not, I think I left one there many years ago," Dad said.

Dad went to search the cabinet. In one drawer he kept some of his junk. After a minute, he came back smiling, a brand-new valve stem in his hand.

"I haven't thought about this piece of metal since I put it in the cabinet. It's a miracle that I remembered it. This has to be God looking after us."

He put the valve stem in the tube and pumped away. It expanded and held the air. Quickly, he deflated the tube so that he could hide it under his jacket until we got to the river.

We were ready.

The artillery pounded and heavy gunfire roared outside. Projectiles exploded around the primary school, the very area we had to pass to get to the river. Even though it was risky to go out, we couldn't wait any longer. We said good-bye to my grandparents. My heart felt as if it were breaking as we left without them.

"If you escape, I could die in peace," Grandpa said in a shaky voice as he closed the door.

The explosions echoed all over the city. We ran behind the garages in our yard and in between my primary school and the city library, stopping here and there to check if anyone was around. I knew the area like the back of my hand. I'd played there with friends throughout my childhood.

We arrived at the riverbank. The night was clear, without clouds. The bright moonlight reflected off the water. A bush grew next to the stairs on the river's edge, and we hid behind it. Only moments later, two Muslim soldiers, in uniforms and with guns in their hands, passed on the road by us. Vlado, believing they had seen him, stepped out and stood next to the bush like he was taking a pee. They saw him but didn't stop or say a word.

"Thank God they didn't suspect anything. It would be such bad luck to die here on the brink of escaping, not even getting into the river," my mom said.

We put the life jackets on. We had to pump the inflatable raft and the tube for my dad. It took us some time because we

Not My Turn to Die

couldn't use the pump on the raft. We had to inflate it by blowing the air from our lungs.

After about ten minutes, Vlado announced, "We're ready. Let's go."

We all made the sign of the cross and said prayers. The moment of truth had come. I looked at my watch. It was 9:20 p.m.

We moved down the stairs. During the summer, the water almost never reaches the stairs. After heavy rains, the river might lap against the third or fourth stair. This time, the water was well past the fifth stair. I'd never seen the Drina this high or this furious.

As soon as I stepped into the water, it felt as if it were cutting into my legs. It was freezing. Still, there was no going back. Between a bullet in my head and swimming in the frigid river, I chose the cold.

"Savo, Sanja, Slobodanka, and I will go first, and we will hold on to the raft. Slavko and Gordana, you wait for a minute and then come after us," Vlado said. "We are more visible and vulnerable if we all go together."

We began our journey to freedom. Our first obstacle were some floats placed all over the river. Because of the shortage of electricity, people had found a way to generate electricity using the river. They created miniturbines on floats that were attached to the bridge by wires. There were dozens of them on the river. We had to make sure to squeeze between them and under the wires.

After some fifty yards, we were under the first bridge. People ran across the bridge from the east to the west bank of the river Drina, oblivious to us swimming below. Many were pushing wheelbarrows with their belongings. I saw their silhouettes before we entered the river. I prayed and hoped the Serbian forces wouldn't shoot on the bridge as we swam under.

Not My Turn to Die

The River Drina: the place where we entered the river to escape.

My prayer was answered. Not one bullet was fired. Between the first and second bridges, I could see and hear massive explosions all over the city. It looked like lightning was constantly striking everywhere.

Seeing that I was shivering, Vlado asked if we were cold.

"I'm not," Sanja said.

"Come on, admit that you are cold. I'm freezing, but I'm also happy we're doing this," I said.

The four of us laughed. Even though it was still a long way to freedom, we were all glad we'd decided to attempt the escape.

We passed another bridge. So far, the current had pushed us along briskly and we didn't have to swim too hard. Beyond the second bridge, the river reached an outcropping of land where the flow slowed down. Some thirty miles down the river

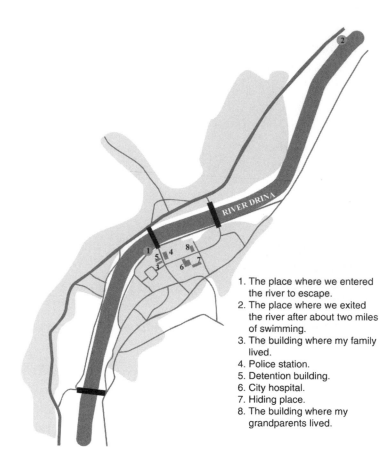

1. The place where we entered the river to escape.
2. The place where we exited the river after about two miles of swimming.
3. The building where my family lived.
4. Police station.
5. Detention building.
6. City hospital.
7. Hiding place.
8. The building where my grandparents lived.

Map showing my family's escape route.

is a large dam built before the war to produce electric power. An artificial lake reaches almost to the city center in Goražde, drastically slowing down the river.

"We'll have to swim harder from here if we don't want to spend hours in this cold water," Slobodanka said.

Vlado said he would push the raft in front of him.

We began swimming.

Not My Turn to Die

Now and then projectiles would explode in the area, flashing bright light for just a moment. Every time, I would on impulse stop swimming and try to cover my head with my hands. A few times, I dipped my head into the river. Luckily, the life jacket wouldn't let me drown.

"How long do we have to do this?" Sanja asked after some time. "I'm getting tired."

"Can you go on for a little while longer?" Vlado asked all of us.

"Let's take a short break before we continue swimming," I said. I had shoes on my feet. The shoes were full of water and felt extremely heavy. It never occurred to me to take them off.

We paused for a few moments, holding on to the inflatable raft. My arms were tired. Still, I didn't want to stop for long.

"Let's keep swimming," Slobodanka said. "When someone needs a break, just say so."

Suddenly, I saw cars driving on the main road coming to Goražde from the north. Their lights were on.

"Those must be Serbs. Muslims would never drive with the lights on. The Serbian snipers and artillery would fire at them immediately," I said.

Vlado looked to the left, then to the right. He was trying to see where we were. He knew the area, he said. He was a fisherman and had often fished around here.

"Let's swim a few more strokes just to be safe. Not far away is the old Serbian Orthodox Church. I heard on the news that that's now a Serbian-controlled area," Vlado said.

After about five minutes, we decided to risk climbing to the shore. I looked at my watch: 10:10 p.m. We'd spent fifty minutes immersed in the icy river. Vlado said we had gone about two miles.

Not My Turn to Die

We waited in the bushes until we caught sight of my parents. We whispered to get their attention, and they heard us. Vlado helped them to get out of the water.

"Let's go to the road and hope that one of those cars with lights on will pass by and see us," Vlado said.

"The Serbian soldiers might think we are a Muslim military unit and kill us before we get a chance to explain who we are," my father said. "We must try to make contact with someone."

We walked along a boardwalk for some time. When we found a pathway heading toward the main road, we followed it.

My clothes clung to my body and I couldn't stop shivering. In our excitement, we had totally forgotten to even take off our life jackets. We carried the inflated floating raft as well.

We trudged about fifty yards along the main road. It was very quiet. We saw no one. Suddenly, a car with its headlights on approached us from the north. According to the news reports from the previous days, this was now Serbian-controlled territory. We stood in the middle of the road, trying to get the driver's attention.

The car stopped about thirty yards away. The lights and the engine went off. Two men hopped out, cocking their guns.

"Who's there? Don't move or we'll fire! Put your hands in the air."

We stood in silence, our hands high in the air, shivering with both cold and fear. *Just give us time to explain,* I thought, my heart racing. *Just give us a second.*

"We escaped from the city. We are Serbs," Vlado said.

"Why should we believe you?"

"We really escaped. See, there are two children with us."

"Is that you, Vlado?" a man asked after a few seconds of silence.

"Yes, it's me," Vlado said, shocked that someone had recognized his voice.

"My God, you are alive," the man said and ran toward us. "We'd heard that you had been killed a long time ago."

They put their machine guns behind their backs and began hugging us. My heart started beating faster than ever before. I was overwhelmed with joy and happiness.

"So, this is it," I said. "We are free. We are finally free!" I wanted to cheer. Then I realized in the last moment that I was still in the middle of nowhere, with fighting not far away.

"You are all wet and shivering. How did you escape?" one of the men asked.

"We swam from the city," my mother said.

Vlado explained to us that the two men were from Goražde and knew him very well. They had been frequent guests in Vlado's restaurant before the war, and had recognized his voice even though they hadn't seen him for two years.

As we talked to the two men, they called for a military truck to come and take us to the Serbian military headquarters established in a nearby suburb. In a flash, I saw about twenty Serbian soldiers appear out of nowhere and surround us.

"You managed to escape from the city? You are all heroes," these soldiers said to us.

I was baffled. "I didn't see anyone seconds ago. Where were you hiding?"

"We were in the bushes. We saw you walking in the middle of the road. If the two children hadn't been with you, we would have fired. You should also thank the two guys who drove by and recognized you," one of the soldiers explained.

"It's a good thing we waited before shooting," another soldier added.

The truck arrived. We scrambled on. We were shivering, but what did it matter? After two years we were finally free.

Many thoughts went through my head as we rode in the back of the truck. At last, I would be able to go to bed at night not fearing that someone might break the door and kill us. I would be able to go wherever I wanted. Sanja and I would go to school again. I would see my relatives after two long years. I wouldn't have to sit in the dark every evening. I would be able to eat as much food as I wanted. I would watch TV and talk on the phone. I would take a real shower again. I couldn't believe it.

The truck arrived at the parking lot of one of the factories in a nearby suburb. There was a large crowd of people in uniforms waiting for our arrival. They had been informed that a truck was coming with a group of Serbs who had escaped from the city.

"Where are the children? Where are Savo and Sanja?" I heard someone pleading. The voice was familiar. It was my father's uncle. The two men who recognized Vlado had talked to him over a two-way radio when they requested a truck to come and pick us up and told him that we escaped. He ran toward us and hugged my sister and me.

"I thought I would never see you again," he said, his voice quavering.

My parents recognized many people there, most of them from Goražde.

"We heard many stories about you being tortured and killed. You are heroes to have survived the two years in the city," one after another person told us.

Suddenly someone said, "Hey, they are wet and shivering. Let them change. We will have time to talk to them later."

We entered a large conference room. Some people brought in uniforms and shirts.

"Change quickly. It would be a pity to get sick now," a woman said to me.

Not My Turn to Die

I tried to take off my clothes but couldn't control my movements. My whole body was shaking. I couldn't even use my hands to unbutton my pants. Someone saw me struggling and came to help me change. The new pants and shirts were an adult size, too big for me, but I didn't mind. I just wanted to be warm again.

The six of us who had escaped together sat in the conference room, surrounded by dozens of people. Everyone wanted to know how we survived and escaped.

"When was the last time you ate?" someone asked.

I couldn't remember. "Early today." It was almost midnight now.

"What do you want to eat? Whatever you ask for, we will get it for you," Dad's uncle said.

"Could I have some bread and chocolate?" I asked.

"May I have an orange?" Sanja said.

My parents, Slobodanka, and Vlado asked if they could have a cup of coffee. Real coffee. Not coffee made out of roasted wheat.

These people brought a loaf of fresh, still-warm bread, a large chocolate bar, and a box full of oranges, bananas, and other fruit. Someone made coffee.

Sanja and I stared at the food. For two years we had dreamed about the food we'd liked to eat before the war. Now people were asking us to say what we'd missed and it would appear on the table.

I loved the smell of the bread on the table in front of me. Someone cut a slice and gave it to me. It was crispy, the way I liked it. I had never before had bread so good.

"I know who would like to hear about your escape the most," Dad's uncle told my mom. "Let's call your sister now." He went to another room and over a two-way radio asked someone to connect him with my mother's sister, who lived in Višegrad, a city twenty-five miles away. When he told her that we'd just escaped from Goražde, she began sobbing, unable to say a word.

It was almost one o'clock in the morning when the people at the headquarters told us that we should get some rest. They took us to abandoned Muslim houses. Vlado, my father, and I slept in a house that had three beds available, while my sister, mom, and Slobodanka went to sleep in another house along with some nurses.

I still heard explosions, since the fighting was continuously going on a few miles away, but I knew I was finally free and safe.

While we slept, all of our relatives throughout Bosnia and Serbia were awakened. My aunt called other family members and told them the news. At first, no one believed her. They had heard many stories about us being tortured and killed, our bodies thrown into the river. Some daily newspapers in Serbia reported once that my grandfather and father had been murdered at the beginning of the war. Propaganda was going full blast on all sides during the war. It didn't seem to be possible that we were alive and safe.

"Has anyone actually seen them? Did anyone talk to them?" my relatives asked.

"Yes, I could hear their voices in the background on the phone but couldn't talk to them at the moment. I just cried," my aunt said.

I was told later that the phones kept ringing all night. Our relatives and friends called one another, celebrating and crying with relief and joy.

———

We found out later that only a day after we'd escaped, a group of Muslim soldiers broke into my home in Goražde. A

Not My Turn to Die

man called Celo, the same man who took my parents hostage on June 18, 1992, led five men, among them Meho, the man who shot at my home and wanted to kill my Grandpa. This marked his fourth attempt to kill my family. He hadn't lied the day before when he told my grandparents that there was a plan to exterminate all Serbs in the city before retreating to the west bank of the river Drina.

My grandparents were in the apartment. When the thugs started breaking in, Grandpa hid behind the bathroom door. Grandma stayed in one of the bedrooms.

"Where are those chetniks, the Heleta family? They can't hide forever. We are going to kill them all," they yelled.

They threw bottles filed with a flammable substance after they broke the door, rapidly setting the apartment on fire. Thinking that my whole family was inside, they had decided to burn us alive.

My grandfather covered himself with wet towels from the bathroom and ran to the balcony. He couldn't go to the stairway of the building because the wild men were at the door, waiting to kill anyone who tried to escape the fire.

Sometimes when people's lives are threatened they are able to have the strength and courage to do things they normally wouldn't be able to do. My Grandpa Nikola, at age sixty-seven, and Grandma Jovanka, at age sixty-five, realized that the only way to survive the fire was to get to our neighbors' apartment over the balcony. They stepped over the second-floor balcony rail and somehow walked on a tiny ledge to reach the balcony of our neighbors. Before the war, my friend Mirza and I sometimes crossed over the balcony fence to get to each other's apartments. I was always afraid of slipping and falling to the ground. I can hardly imagine my grandparents managing this, but that's how they survived. Our neighbor Amra told them to hide in one of her bedrooms. When the terror squad suspected the escape and wanted to search her apartment, Amra courageously stood at the door and refused to let them in.

The fire started to spread, making the men impatient. Once they moved away from Amra's door, my grandparents covered themselves with blankets and walked out of our neighbors' home. It was a moment of total chaos because all of the neighbors were trying to escape the fire, which was quickly spreading beyond my home. With their faces hidden under the blankets, my grandparents were able to slip by the soldiers who were waiting in the stairway, watching our door to see if any of our family would still come out of the burning apartment. My grandparents passed by Meho, who stood in the stairway, his gun pointed at our door, yelling that they should wait until our apartment burned down and then enter it to make sure we were all dead.

In the yard, my grandparents found other Serbs who lived in the same building. They all desperately needed to find a place to hide.

"Let's go to the police station," someone suggested. "We should ask them to help us, even though they have never done so in the past. We don't have any other options."

Luckily, in the deserted police station, they found two policemen who had been good friends of my father and my uncles when they were children.

"Nikola, many people want to kill Serbs tonight. We can't protect you. We can only lock you in our jail until the situation calms down," one of the policemen said.

"We have nowhere to go. Please take us to the cells," my grandfather said.

About ten of them spent that night in jail. The police gave them two old mats, a few blankets, and a bucket of water. In the morning, the police escorted them to the house of our friend Vlado. His mother and uncle were still in the city, opening their house to dozens of Serbs who had nowhere to go.

Blinded by hatred, people will go to extremes to kill. The terror squad burned my home, which was located in the middle of the building and surrounded by apartments where our Muslim neighbors lived. The blaze spread to the apartment above, where a Muslim woman and her children lived. Neighbors had to enter the burning apartment and save the three small children from being burned alive. In order to kill my family, Celo, Meho, and the three monsters who came with them didn't mind killing Muslim children too.

The Serbian military action on Goražde stopped on April 24, after long negotiations with the United Nations. The UN troops entered the city that same evening. Serbs never conquered Goražde during the war in Bosnia. Despite millions of bullets and tens of thousands of shells and projectiles fired on the city and its defenses, Goražde didn't give in.

10

Soon after escaping from Goražde, we had to start adjusting to normal life. My family stayed with our relatives in Višegrad, a city in the Serbian-controlled part of Bosnia. Sanja and I immediately went back to primary school. The school board in Višegrad wanted to help us catch up with our peers. Over two months, we studied hard and took many exams in order to finish fifth and seventh grade, respectively. In the end, we were only one year behind.

The war still ravaged Bosnia. For months, my dad and his two brothers tried everything they could to get my grandparents out of Goražde. Finally, with the help of the UN forces, my grandparents were able to leave the city in November 1994. In return, the Serbian officials secured a safe passage for two Muslim surgeons from Sarajevo to Goražde.

After finishing primary school in 1995, I started high school in Višegrad. My high school professors were underpaid, and many didn't really care about the quality of education they provided. Many times our male teachers had to leave and fight in the war, so we missed weeks of classes. Some of the teachers expressed their growing frustration by beating students. Our English-language teachers soon realized that they could make more money if they worked as translators for the UN forces. They left us. From then on we had no English classes. Once a semester, the school hired someone to come for a day and give us passing grades, making our "progress" look official.

I was happy to be free. No one was threatening to kill my family any more. My human rights were respected. I wasn't hungry. I had electricity and running water. I could go to school like other kids. Nevertheless, life was far from perfect. My family didn't have a home. Višegrad, the city where we were staying, used to have a Muslim majority. When the war began, the Muslim residents had been forced out of their homes and the city. Many were killed. Serbs who had been forced to leave their homes in the Muslim- and Croatian-controlled territories all over Bosnia now occupied Muslim houses in Višegrad. My parents tried to rent housing in the city, but without success.

In late 1995, my family moved to Kopači, a suburb near Goražde that was controlled by Serbs. The lawlessness we'd experienced in Muslim-controlled Goražde during the war had continued in the Serbian-controlled territory but in reverse. I saw Muslim houses in Kopači being raided and looted by Serbs. A number of houses had been burned down after all the valuables had been stolen.

In Kopači, we found one such empty house a Muslim family had been forced to flee in 1994. The house lacked windows, doors, and furniture. My parents and I found some old couches, beds, doors, tables, and cabinets left abandoned around raided houses. Since we had nothing, we took them. With a little cleaning and repairs, the furniture we'd scavenged was usable.

My mother was unemployed, while my father worked as a journalist. The money he received for his work often wasn't

My dad, mom, sister, and I with our relatives a
month after our escape in 1994.

My dad in 1995.   My mom in 1995.

enough to buy food. We had a small garden where we planted vegetables. All four of us worked in the garden almost every afternoon, growing food and trying to save what little money my dad was making for other necessities.

In December 1995, the civil war in Bosnia and Herze-govina ended with the Dayton Peace Accords. The country was officially divided into two, and unofficially into three, homo-geneous ethnic parts. Serbs retained their own entity. Croats and Muslims share another entity only on paper, since in real-ity, they are segregated along ethnic lines. The nationalists who had triggered the bloodshed, backed by the Western world, remained in power long after the war had formally ended.

In the aftermath of the war, I regularly considered hurting and even killing those responsible for my suffering. Two years after our escape, the wounds were still fresh. I was free, but I still had painful memories that wouldn't go away. I thought that revenge was the only way to move forward with my life.

I dreamed about punishing those who enjoyed terrorizing my family. I wanted to see them suffering, crying for mercy. I wanted them to feel how I felt for two years.

Only months after the war ended, Muslim convoys began driving between Goražde and the Bosnian capital of Sarajevo through Serbian-controlled territory. My Serbian friends and I soon started attacking these convoys with rocks. We looked like the Palestinian youth in the West Bank and Gaza fighting the Israelis. We would hide in the bushes near the main road and wait for the Muslim trucks and buses. We had masks on our faces and rocks in our hands. A few times we completely smashed windshields on trucks and side windows on buses.

I considered slinging rocks as a partial payback for everything my family and I had undergone in Goražde. It hardly crossed my mind at the time that perhaps those people in the buses and trucks had not done anything bad to my family. Some of them could even have been those who had helped us. Maybe even the man who gave us his last loaf of bread. I was completely blinded by fury.

Because of such attacks, the NATO forces began escorting the convoys. NATO soldiers accompanied drivers while their armored vehicles drove in front and back of the convoys. My friends and I stopped our attacks but secretly planned future retaliation.

It was in one of these convoys that I found him. Meho.

He was free. He seemed confident that nothing bad would ever happen to him. He even had NATO soldiers on his side, assuring his safety.

I was outraged. I just wanted to kill him. I didn't care about consequences. All I could think about was this madman entering my home and pointing a machine gun at my family. I kept imagining him with a gun pointed at the line of people, including my grandfather. I pictured him firing at my home. I imagined the wild expression on his face when he burned my home and said that they must make sure we were all dead.

My friends and I got a handgun and a grenade from a friend who lived nearby. I told them I didn't care about anyone else in the convoy. I only wanted to kill this monster. I wanted to kill him with joy.

Not My Turn to Die

I checked to make sure that the bullet was in the gun barrel. I covered the gun with the sleeve of my shirt.

We weren't far away from the trucks when I saw my dad running down the street toward me. Someone who had heard me yelling at Meho went to tell him about my fury. Afraid I would do something bad after seeing the man who had oppressed us, he had set out to find me.

I paused and waited for him. I didn't want him to watch. I wanted him to go back and let me do what I needed to do. My friends moved away, leaving me to talk to my father.

"Savo, what are you doing? Stop and talk to me."

"Why did you have to come now? I don't want to talk to you. There's something I've got to do." I tried to sound resolved.

"What do you intend to do?"

"There he is, in one of the trucks. It's Meho," I pointed with my empty hand. "I'm going to kill him. He'll pay for all the suffering and pain he caused us."

My father saw that I was hiding something in my sleeve.

"What is that? Is that a gun?"

"Yes. I'm going to do it, no matter what you have to say," I said.

"Please don't kill him. You have your life ahead of you. You are only seventeen."

"What life? Living next to those who wanted to kill us? Seeing them walking around free?"

"You have had enough horror in your life," my father said. "Do you want to go to jail after you kill him?"

"I don't care about jail," I said. "He tried to kill us. He shot at us. He wanted to burn us alive. I can't sleep without him bursting in on my dreams. He has to die."

"It would be even worse if you kill him. You'll only have more nightmares."

Not My Turn to Die

"If you can live with the fact that he is here free, you go on. I can't," I told my dad. "When I punish him, I'll be able to move on with my life. Please leave now. Let me do this."

Dad continued talking. "Killing or torturing him or anybody else will never erase your memories or bring you a brighter future. You will only become another murderer. I'm telling you this because I love you and want the best for you. Don't lose your own humanity by taking anyone's life."

I didn't know what to say. I looked at my father. I wanted to cry. I wished the war was just a bad dream, that it had never happened.

"I would never kill another human being," I said. "But, Meho, he is a monster. He is not human."

"You say he is a monster for terrorizing us. Don't become a monster like him."

"This won't make me a monster," I tried to explain. "Revenge is the only way I can continue with life."

"Accomplish something in your life. Be a good person and don't hate anyone. Let that be your revenge. Show them that they couldn't break you," Dad said.

I looked at the gun in my hand, then into my father's eyes, and, finally, toward the truck where Meho was still sitting.

"We don't want to lose you," my father added, sensing the emotional conflict deep in my mind.

I thought about my parents. They felt responsible and guilty for staying in Goražde with my sister and me. They had watched us starving and suffering. Now that we were free again, they struggled to make our lives better. The worst thing in the world for them would be to now lose Sanja or me. If I were to kill Meho, I would probably go to jail.

Do I want to do this to my parents? By killing this monster, I would also certainly kill something vital in my mom and dad. If they had had to, they would have died for my sister and me. They wanted us to be good people. I couldn't crush their hopes and destroy their lives.

Do I want to become a murderer? Hadn't I suffered enough? Hadn't I had enough of gloom and despair? Would killing him really make me happy? Would killing him really erase the past suffering?

I lowered the gun. My father stepped closer and I handed it to him. Drained, I immediately started walking home. My father followed me.

The days after the incident at the convoy were emotionally very difficult for me. I questioned my decision to walk away and let the man who wanted to kill my family go free. Still, in the end, my love for my family prevailed over my hatred toward my oppressors. I envisioned doing something that would make my family proud instead of adding misery to their lives.

My parents helped me go through the battle that was raging in my mind and heart by spending a lot of time talking to me about the uselessness of violence and revenge. They didn't want me to be volatile and lose control again at the sight of someone who had terrorized us during the war. After these conversations, I saw those who had tried to kill my family many times. Even though I didn't want to hurt them anymore, I did imagine seeing them being held responsible for their actions.

Watching them remain free and as ignorant as ever was something I couldn't justify. Within only a couple of years after the end of the war, these thugs started freely coming to the Serbian-controlled part of Bosnia where we lived as if they had

Not My Turn to Die

never done anything bad to anyone. The local Serbian police officials knew about their deeds. My parents, like many other Serbian adults who were oppressed in Goražde, had provided long interviews to the police, including details and names of the tormenters. Still, for some reason, the Serbian police never arrested these criminals, nor did they even question them.

Where was the justice and fairness I'd been raised to count on? There was no justice in Goražde or anywhere else in the country during the war. Now, to my surprise, there was no justice in Bosnia after the war either. And there was little hope for better tomorrow.

11

After the war, Bosnia was in ruins, the economy was devastated, and hundreds of thousands of people misplaced. Around 100,000 people died in the war. Even the centuries-old monuments, countless graveyards, tombstones, and sacred religious buildings had been destroyed by the extremists on all sides.

So many wounds remained open. So much hatred simmered. People were unsatisfied and bitter. They had been brainwashed that they had to fight so they could live better lives. After the war, many came to realize how miserable and ugly their lives had become.

Most of the refugees and displaced people never went back to their homes. Trust was lost during the war and people decided to stay in areas where their ethnic groups were now in majority. After getting back their homes and properties, or what was left of them, people would sell or exchange them and move to other parts of the country.

My parents briefly returned to Goražde, to our home, that was renovated after being burned down in 1994. They didn't want to go back, but they had to live in it for a few months in order to sell it. The international community's administrators who now practically governed Bosnia came up with that rule. They didn't care how their decisions would affect people who not long ago went through hell.

Even though no one threatened them any more, these few months were emotionally very painful for my parents. My sister and I were away for most of the time, but Mom and Dad had to be around those same people who took them hostage, who arrested and detained us, who forced my dad to clean city streets and do hard labor, the same people who fired their guns at us and called us animals. Even the former city mayor, the man who signed our arrest warrants and who ordered our detention and who according to many ordered killings of dozens of Serbian civilians in Goražde during the war, came back after a diplomatic career and was welcomed as a distinguished citizen.

As soon as my parents spent required time in the apartment and got all the paperwork done, they exchanged our home with a Muslim family who had a similar apartment in Visegrad, a city with a Serbian majority some 25 miles from Goražde. They are trying to rebuild their lives from scratch, like hundreds of thousands of other people in Bosnia and Herzegovina. My mom remained unemployed, while my dad spent time working as a journalist and writing poetry for children.

I was very pessimistic about my future. I often wondered why we stayed in Bosnia. We could have also emigrated like our friends Slobodanka, Dragan, and many others. After escaping from Goražde, they decided that they had enough of Bosnia and emigrated with their families to Canada or the United States.

I finished high school having missed half of my classes. I missed some because my teachers weren't there and some because I saw no point in attending an unorganized educational institution. I dreamed of making something of myself, but I had no means to go to college. My parents couldn't help me. My Dad was working hard, yet he was underpaid for the work he was doing. My sister went to college in Serbia to study arts and design. Our parents couldn't financially afford educating both of us.

I had to find a job in a country where half of the population was unemployed.

Looking around for opportunities, I met some young people who worked in local youth organizations established after the war. They often received funds from international donors to work on peacemaking and community development projects. They encouraged me to get involved. I did since I had nothing else to do.

Soon, I found myself attending seminars and conferences. I began traveling and meeting dozens of young people from all over Bosnia. In the beginning, I found it a bit awkward to talk to Muslims and Croats. Many of us felt that though the war had ended there still existed barriers for an open conversation. However, after a while, we all realized that we didn't have to blindly hang on to the past. We could respect each other and cooperate.

People I met seemed enthusiastic and optimistic about the future, increasing my own confidence. I became involved in a number of educational projects aimed at young people, spreading the message about the importance of inter-ethnic dialogue and voting.

One day, a friend faxed me an application for a youth program in the United States.

"I can't even read this," I told to my friend over the phone. "It's all in English."

"Do you know any English?"

"I can understand a bit, but I don't know enough to read or to have a conversation. We barely had English in high school. I can't fill in this application on my own."

"Well, think about it and if you are interested, find someone to help you," my friend said.

The date of the deadline was approaching and I still hadn't even read the application. I called a friend of mine who was a translator for the UN forces. In a coffee shop, she read the application.

"This sounds great! The Institute for Multi-Track Diplomacy from Washington, DC, is looking for a diverse group of youth from Bosnia and Herzegovina. They want to take them to Minnesota and Canada for camping and canoeing, and then to Minneapolis and Washington, DC, for community development training. All expenses are paid. They are looking for 36 young people," my friend summarized the application for me.

"Hundreds of people will apply. They will never pick me," I said.

"It's not going to hurt if you try. Let's fill this in right now."

After we completed the application, I told my friend, "It's probably a waste of time, but if I'm going to do it I only have an hour to fax this. I better go now."

I sent the application, but didn't expect anything to happen.

A week after I applied, I got a phone call to come for an interview. I couldn't believe they wanted to talk to me. I was puzzled.

I went to Banjaluka, a city in northern Bosnia. The interview took place in a house where the partner NGO had its offices. I met some local people and a few Americans. I didn't know anyone there.

A man in his thirties called my name. It was time for my interview. I felt extremely nervous. I believe the people who sat on the other side of the table saw the sweat on my forehead. My voice quavered. It was the first formal interview in my life.

They asked me about my previous experience in community development and youth projects. They wanted to know if I was interested in doing more for my community and if I was willing to commit to the program for a year. I told them about seminars I had attended, volunteering at the radio station where my father worked, and explained my roles in projects that encouraged youth to get involved in the election process.

"I might not have a lot of experience, but I'm willing to learn and commit myself to this program," I concluded, finally somewhat calmed by the end of the interview.

"You'll be informed if you are chosen to be a participant by the end of next week," the woman interviewer said.

I returned home. My parents and my friends asked how the interview had gone.

"I don't know what to tell you. I was so nervous. I don't expect them to pick me. There must have been so many people with better qualifications."

Days passed slowly. About a week after the interview I was on my way home for lunch when I saw my mother standing outside the house, smiling and holding a piece of paper.

"You better hurry. I have great news for you!"

"What is it?"

"You got a call today. They have picked you. You'll go to America! They said you have to go to Sarajevo and bring your passport and some other papers to apply for the American and Canadian visas. Here is a phone number you should call," my mother said, handing me the paper.

I stared at it. Yes, there was the phone number and everything else my mother had just told me. "Please tell me you are not joking."

"Just call that number and you will see it's true," Mom said. "I wouldn't joke about this."

I was dumbfounded. I couldn't believe they had chosen me over more than four hundred young people that had applied from all over Bosnia. I was one of thirty-six.

I can't blow this opportunity, I thought. I have to make the most of it.

The next year had an enormous influence on me. I met thirty-five young people from all over Bosnia and Herzegovina, Muslims, Croats, and Serbs. Many of them had suffered during the war. We didn't want to talk about the conflict that had ended only three years before. Some of our American mentors encouraged us to discuss the war in our country, but the majority of us refused. We had had enough of the war and its darkness. We wanted to move on and do something positive for ourselves and our communities.

We traveled to the United States, spending time in northern Minnesota, parts of Canada, Minneapolis, and Washington, DC. That was the first time I'd traveled beyond the borders of the former Yugoslavia. I was truly impressed by the United States, the beautiful nature in Minnesota, the skyscrapers in Minneapolis, and the museums and monuments in D.C. We'd met many great people but also encountered many ignorant ones who thought that we were savages who knew nothing about the modern world. To our amazement, many of those people were educated individuals, some even professors from universities in Minneapolis and Saint Paul that we met at the reception that Jesse Ventura, the Minnesota governor at the time, had organized for us. They only knew about Bosnia what the American media had told them over the years. They had asked us if we had cars in Bosnia, if we have ever seen a color TV before, if we'd known what a washing machine was. . . . We laughed at their questions and those who spoke English often offered the most ridiculous answers.

Americans we met were asking us about post-traumatic stress and if we had undergone counseling after the war. Those in our group who could speak English tried to explain that the majority of people in Bosnia and Herzegovina don't like to talk about emotional problems and feelings to strangers. We have family and friends for that.

Back in Bosnia, in the program—officially named Peace-Trails—we learned about community development, leadership, writing projects and budget proposals, and each got an opportunity to work on our own project in our communities. My project was to organize meetings and conferences between youth organizations from different parts of Bosnia and Herzegovina. The goal was to get young people to talk to each other and plan peace building projects together. The project was very successful, connecting many young people from all sides.

After a year as a participant, I was offered a job at Peace-Trails. I was delighted by the offer and immediately accepted the job.

I had more responsibilities now as a program coordinator, working with new participants. I traveled all over Bosnia and Herzegovina, visiting many places for the first time in my life. I was now in the team with the people who had interviewed me and picked me over hundreds of others. I wanted to know why.

"We could feel the energy and sense your potential," one of the coworkers told me. "You said you wanted to learn, do something positive, and work with other young people. That was the profile we'd been looking for."

In the second year of the program's existence, The Institute for Multi-Track Diplomacy pulled out of PeaceTrails. However, The Whalen Family Foundation from Oakland, California, that provided funding for the program from the beginning, continued to help PeaceTrails. In the second year, Daniel Whalen, the foundation's president, became closely involved in the program's development.

Unlike the majority of the international donors who came to "civilize" us and show us how we were supposed to live, work, and think, Mr. Whalen always said that it was us, the local staff from Bosnia, who should have a say in making plans and decisions about projects because we knew what our country and its people needed. Not him or any other foreigner.

While in PeaceTrails, I was surrounded by positive people who weren't preoccupied with nationalism and the war. Going home after our meetings was often a totally different experience. My parents told me about some of our new Serbian neighbors coming to them and telling them to prevent me from "working with the enemy." Many times I've heard people shouting "traitor" after me, some even saying it in my face. I didn't care. I laughed at these comments. I knew I wasn't betraying anybody. I was only trying to do something good for myself and others.

Through some of my friends from PeaceTrails, my sister Sanja got involved in a project called Balkan Youth Voices. The aim of the project was to help youth work together through music. With ten other young people from Bosnia and Herzegovina, she traveled to New York City in August 2000. They spent a month there, practicing chorus and performing. They even sang at the United Nations headquarters.

I was able to persuade a few of my Serbian friends to get involved in similar youth programs. However, many didn't want to change. They remained narrow-minded and under the

Savo standing in front of the Statue of Liberty.

My sister Sanja (right) and a friend in New York in September 2000.

influence of nationalistic propaganda. This happened to many on all sides. A large percentage of youth stayed trapped in the net of intolerance and hate.

After two years in PeaceTrails, my friends from the staff and I traveled to Hawaii and San Francisco. This was our annual reward trip.

My friends and I were thrilled when we arrived in Hawaii. Every single person in the local PeaceTrails staff had gone through some bad times during the war. We couldn't believe that now, in February 2002, we were in this paradise.

"I don't think it could get better than this," one of my friends said to me in one of the colorful Hawaiian restaurants overlooking the blue ocean.

"I don't think so either," I replied.

The next evening my Bosnian friends and I met with Mr. Whalen and his staff.

"I'm delighted to have you working for PeaceTrails," Mr. Whalen said. "But tonight, I would like you to stop thinking about your job. I want you to think about your dreams. What would you like to be in the future? What would you like to do in your lives? Dream! Don't think that something is unrealistic. Please dream big!"

We were speechless. No one ever expected to hear anything like this.

Mr. Whalen continued: "I would like to talk about your dreams with all of you individually when we arrive in San Francisco next week. Please don't be shy about revealing them. Think about the greatest things you would like to do. I want to know if I can help you reach your dreams."

I couldn't believe what I had just heard. Mr. Whalen wanted to help us realize our dreams. Up until this moment, I'd thought that people dream big dreams, but then wake up in the real world.

What do I hope to do in my life? What is my greatest dream? I enjoyed working for PeaceTrails. I was able to meet amazing people, travel, work on a variety of projects, and learn about community development, communication, and peace building. Still, I felt I could do more.

I asked myself for days what I would tell Mr. Whalen when I sit down to talk to him. I could tell him that I'd always wanted to go to college, but had never had the opportunity. But how could I possibly ask for anything? I had found a great job thanks to him. I had traveled around the world thanks to him. My life had gone in a totally positive direction since my involvement with PeaceTrails.

I decided not to make any decisions before I meet with Mr. Whalen. I'd see how the meeting goes and sense if I dared tell him I dream of going to college.

I couldn't sleep the night before the meeting. We were in a downtown San Francisco hotel, a block from Chinatown. I spent the day wandering around the city by myself, deep in thought.

After dinner, I met with Mr. Whalen in a corner of the hotel's lobby. A friend of mine came with me to help me with the English translation. My English wasn't good enough to converse easily on my own and this was a very important moment in my life.

I thanked him for taking us to see an NBA game a few days before, my long lasting wish. We had watched the Sacramento Kings, my favorite NBA team, playing the Indiana Pacers. The Pacers had won but it was still fun, especially since we had tickets for the third row. I couldn't believe my eyes when I saw Vlade Divac and Predrag Stojakovic, two Serbs playing for the Kings, waving at me and saying hello. They recognized the jersey of Divac's former team from Belgrade that I had been wearing.

Finally, Mr. Whalen asked me about my greatest dream.

Nervously moving in the chair, I tried to say something, but, at first, the words wouldn't come. Then I finally said: "I've

Not My Turn to Die

thought about my dreams since our conversation in Hawaii. I don't think it would be fair to ask you to do anything more for me. At one point, my life was a complete mess. It totally changed after I got involved with PeaceTrails. I have a great job now. With your help, I've traveled all over the world."

"Please don't think that way," Mr. Whalen said. "Forget for a moment what I've done. What do you want to do in your life? Who do you want to become? I would be happy to help you if you want to do something else."

A real battle was going on inside my head. Should I say that I would like to go to college or should I say that I appreciate what he had done for me and couldn't ask for more? I had to say something soon.

"Well, there is something . . . I . . . I would like to go to college. I always wanted to go to college but couldn't afford it. I had to work. My parents weren't able to help me. That . . . that is my greatest dream."

Pressure, like the weight of a mountain, left my heart. I looked at Mr. Whalen. He was smiling.

"Thank you for telling me that. I'll help you go to college. Any one, anywhere! I'll pay for your education."

I couldn't believe what I had just heard. I fully expected to wake up and realize that I had been dreaming. It can't be that simple, I thought to myself. I just told Mr. Whalen about a dream I never expected to come true, and he told me without any hesitation to pick a college anywhere in the world. He didn't even take time to think about it. He just said yes.

I reached for a glass of water sitting on the table in front of me and took a sip. It tasted like real water. I looked around the room. This was really happening.

"When I was growing up, my family wasn't wealthy. I would not be able to go to college without the help from others. I now want to help people like you," Mr. Whalen said. "Take time and think about where you would like to go to school, but not a lot of time. You need to apply soon, to begin your college education in the fall."

"I can start college this year?"

"Yes, you have enough time to apply. Did you ever think about the school you would like to attend?"

"Not really. I never thought I would get the opportunity. Still, I remember you telling us about Saint John's University in Minnesota, where you received your undergraduate degree. You said it was a great school for you so I believe it would be a great school for me. If it's possible, I'd like to go there. I'm only worried about my English."

"You'll have to study English over the summer. Don't worry about that now. I'd be happy if you chose St. John's over other great colleges. It is a great place, indeed. You would have a great experience there and your life would completely change," Mr. Whalen told me.

That night, and many times later, I thought about my life and how it would turn out if I had chosen different paths in the past. What if I hadn't listened when my father told me not to kill the man who had terrorized us during the war? What if I had never sent in my application for PeaceTrails? What if . . . ?

Between the dark and the light, I'd chosen the light. Luckily, I'd chosen hope!

———

Before I went to Minnesota to attend a school for English language for two months prior to going to St. John's, my friend and I met with Mr. Whalen. She, too, had worked for Peace-

Not My Turn to Die

Trails and her dream was to go to college in the United States. Her dream, too, became a reality.

We wanted to know if and how we would return the funds invested in our education.

"How could we return what you are doing for us? Do you have any requests?" my friend asked.

Mr. Whalen smiled: "No, I don't have any formal requests. Still, there is something I want to ask you. If you are ever in a situation to help someone in any way, please do it. You don't have to do it for me, do it for yourself."

My friend and I looked at each other, puzzled. How's this possible? A man is giving us a new life, brighter future, education, great opportunities, and in return wants nothing for himself.

I spent the first two months in the United States in St. Paul, Minnesota, attending school for English. I always knew that my English was bad and that I would have a hard time at college, but I found my life now way more frustrating than I expected it to be.

I lived with an American family that had four little sons. I tried to talk to them, but could hardly have a simple conversation even with the boys.

At school, I could understand some English, but had a hard time speaking and expressing myself. I could barely write anything. One of my teachers assigned us to read *Newsweek* as a way of learning the language and new terms. I would read articles and write down what I understood was their main point. It always turned out that I was wrong.

Like me, my classmates were beginners trying to learn

English. One day, one of the teachers asked us about our plans for the future. A few of us said we were going to attend American colleges.

"I don't want to discourage you, but you should know that, with this level of English, you are not ready for an American college education. Even American students often find it difficult," teacher told us.

I'll make it somehow, even if I don't sleep at all, I thought. I couldn't say it out loud. I didn't know how.

———

During my first semester at St. John's University I was mostly quiet, trying to understand what was going on in my classes. Even when I would understand what my professors were asking, I would not know how to answer. After classes, I hardly spoke to anyone apart from a few Bosnian friends who came to study with me. Mr. Whalen provided them, too, with full scholarships.

At this time, dictionary was my best friend. I had to use it to understand what I was reading or to find appropriate words to express myself in writing. Often, I felt like my head would explode in the early morning hours, but I never thought about giving up. I wanted to make up for all those lost years.

I realized that I had to vent my frustration somehow so I began running in the college cross country team. This helped me to meet new people and take my stressed mind away for a moment.

I only felt comfortable in my English class, where I and other foreign students worked on improving our reading, writing, and conversational skills. Sarah Pruett, our professor, was a very patient teacher. Unlike the teacher from St. Paul who didn't believe I would make it at an American college, Sarah always believed in all of us. Without her help, most of us foreign students would probably never accomplish anything at school.

She helped us with reading and pronunciation and encouraged us to take part in class discussion. She told us to read a lot. She said that it would help us increase our vocabulary. I read all the time. Books, newspapers, anything I could find. Sarah also worked with us on our writing assignments for other classes, never refusing to read our papers before we had to submit them.

With every passing week, I found it easier to write in English, but I still struggled with speaking. It was easier to express myself on paper. I didn't have to worry about pronunciation.

My second semester was easier than the first one. I now felt more comfortable speaking English. I wasn't afraid to voice my opinion in class anymore.

I met a lot of new friends from all over the world—India, Zimbabwe, Nigeria, Ireland, Trinidad, to name only a few. And of course Americans. They all brought something new into my life, a new story, perspective, opinion. They all helped me grow.

Anywhere I went at St. Benedict and St. John's, two schools sharing one academic program, I felt at home. Whenever I needed help, there were people going an extra mile to help me. If they couldn't help, they still had kind words of support and encouragement. This meant a lot.

I soon realized a whole new world full of hope opening in front of me. I found support, people who believed in me and cared about my future. I found professors and fellow students who welcomed and respected my opinions even when they were contrary to their own. They challenged me to open my mind, grow, stretch my horizons, dream big, and become a better and more tolerant person.

I found everything I had dreamed about!

At school, I enjoyed the fact that I could explore with different classes and find a major that suited me. I first decided to major in business management. I liked the practical side of it.

Since St. John's is a liberal arts university, we all had to take a variety of classes outside our majors. After I took a few history classes to fulfill my humanities requirement, I knew I had to study history too, so I added another major. I began focusing on African and particularly South African history after a Sub-Saharan African history class. I was fascinated that, even though South Africa had one of the most troublesome and inhumane histories in the world, it was nevertheless able to end apartheid relatively peacefully at the same time the war was ravaging my country. Above all, I was captivated by Nelson Mandela who spent twenty-seven years in prison and came out not hating anyone, but went on spreading a message of peace and reconciliation.

When I was told that I could study abroad for a semester, I knew where I would go. My only choice was South Africa.

Once, in Cape Town, I got to meet two former Robben Island prisoners. I asked them, "How do you feel today? Is it hard to see those who oppressed you walking around free?"

"There is no anger in me," one of them said. "I fought to be respected as a human being in my own country. In 1994, black South Africans voted for the first time in their lives. We are free now."

Another man added: "Racial laws are abolished. We got what we were fighting for. We got our freedom. I'm not angry at

Not My Turn to Die

the whites who had terrorized me. I moved on for the sake of the future."

From the moment when these two men shook my hand, I couldn't stop thinking about what they had said. Here were people terrorized since birth, but they still hadn't sought revenge. They were able to reconcile with their horrific past for the sake of the future.

For a long time after the war, I considered reconciliation as a weakness. I saw revenge as the only way, the "manly" way to move on with my life. But with the help of my family, and after my life changed for the better and I got exposed to education and traveled all over the world, I realized that was wrong. I realized that only brave and strong people can put years of suffering behind them, reconcile with the past, and move on with life. I wanted to be one of them.

Shortly after the encounter with the two former Robben Island prisoners, my American friends asked me for the first time about my wartime experience in Bosnia. When I told them about it, they began persuading me to write about it. I didn't believe anyone would ever read it, but writing helped me deal with everything that had happened.

———

My greatest dream became reality in May 2006, when I graduated from Saint John's University. My sister also graduated from college in Belgrade, Serbia, majoring in graphic design.

After college, I returned to South Africa. I had my personal reasons, but I also wanted to continue education and get a Masters Degree in conflict transformation and management from Nelson Mandela Metropolitan University in Port Elizabeth. I want to work in this field and perhaps contribute to conflict

Savo and Daniel Whalen at Savo's graduation in 2006.

resolution around the world. I realize that conflict is a part of human relations but I also believe that if managed well, it doesn't have to be as destructive as the war in Bosnia was in the 1990s.

Epilogue

I 've learned a lot in the past years. I've learned to appreciate all the things I used to take for granted. Freedom, security, food, friendship. I've learned about the importance of family. Without their help I would never have taken the right paths. They gave me support when I didn't see any hope and encouraged me to choose reconciliation.

I came to believe that God, or some divine power, indeed exists. This didn't come to me after going to church or reading the Bible. It came after, over and over again, my family was saved when we were on the edge of death. It came after we got our freedom back. It came through the individuals who were there for us when we needed help the most. Yet I never understood why I was saved when many others weren't. Perhaps, it simply was not my turn to die.

I realize that what happened in Bosnia could happen anywhere in the world, particularly in places that are diverse and have a history of conflict. It only takes bad leadership for a *country to go up in flames, for people of different ethnicity, color, or religion to kill each other as if they had nothing in common whatsoever. Having a democratic constitution, laws that secure human rights, police that maintain order, a judicial system, and freedom of speech don't ultimately guarantee long lasting peace. If greedy or bloodthirsty leaders come to power, it all can go down. It happened to us. It can happen to you.*

In every war and on every side, there are those who hate, those who don't care, and there are good people. Helped by the good people, brave and caring individuals, both known and unknown to my family, we survived the horrors of the war and starvation. I came to realize that a single person can often make a difference between life and death, hope and despair. The people who helped my family would never admit they did anything special when they helped us. After the war, my mother gave thanks to some of them for all they had done for us; they didn't believe that their caring gestures were out of the ordinary. And yet a loaf of bread, a hiding place, or a word of support, again and again, made the difference for us.

I had great parents who spent a lot of time urging me to remain a good person and never hurt another human being. When I was lost and thought that bloody revenge was the only way to move forward with my life, I was lucky to be surrounded by the people who had helped me never to give up on the promise of a better life.

Many people in Bosnia, including a number of my friends, didn't experience such support. They gave up. They got lost. Many never found a way to escape the clutches of hatred. Many couldn't live under the pressure and, like some of my very close friends, committed suicide.

In the summer of 2003, I went back to Bosnia to visit my family and friends during the summer break from college. One day I was in a café with some of my friends when I saw a man called Celo, the man who during the war had taken my parents hostage and burned our home thinking we were inside. Most of my companions didn't know details about my wartime experience. They noticed that I changed my mood. I stopped laughing and sat silent, gazing through a window at the green Bosnian hills in the distance.

After insisting to know what suddenly went wrong, one of my friends who knew explained: "See the skinny guy with the short brown hair? He wanted to kill Savo and his family in Goražde. He burned their home."

My friends couldn't believe I was able to sit there, quiet and composed.

"I would kill the bastard with my bare hands," one of them said.

But I didn't hate him anymore. I didn't want to hurt him in any way. I had finally made peace with the past. I didn't care that he was free, never even questioned for his crimes. I just didn't want to see him and be reminded of the evil that some people are capable of.

One of my Serbian friends wanted to bring me a handgun from his car. When I refused, he began pestering me: "Come on! Ask me and I kill him for you. It will be my pleasure. Muslims killed my father during the war. Just nod and leave. I'll do it. I'm leaving Bosnia tomorrow and no one will ever find me."

"Please don't do anything. This is between me and him. If I wanted revenge, I'd hurt or kill him myself," I said.

I called over the café bar owner and asked him if he could

Sanja, Gordana, Savo, and Slavko Heleta.

tell Celo and his friends to leave before things got out of control. When they left, I tried to explain to my friends why I had react-ed the way I did. I told them I didn't want to be like those who had attempted to murder my family. Would someone's pain, someone's blood on my hands, erase my wartime memories and make my life better? I wanted to be better than them. I wanted to live a life where I can look in the mirror every day and not regret the things I've done. I wanted to be a good human being for I know the gruesomeness that bad people bring about.

I had made peace with the past. And I was looking toward the future.